Leadership in Energy and Environmental Design

LEED® NC
Practice Problems

New Construction

Meghan Peot, MEd and
Brennan Schumacher, LEED AP

Professional Publications Inc. • Belmont, CA

How to Locate and Report Errata for This Book

At Professional Publications, we do our best to bring you error-free books. But when errors do occur, we want to make sure you can view corrections and report any potential errors you find, so the errors cause as little confusion as possible.

A current list of known errata and other updates for this book is available on the PPI website at **www.ppi2pass.com/errata**. We update the errata page as often as necessary, so check in regularly. You will also find instructions for submitting suspected errata. We are grateful to every reader who takes the time to help us improve the quality of our books by pointing out an error.

LEED NC PRACTICE PROBLEMS: NEW CONSTRUCTION

Current printing of this edition: 4

Printing History

edition number	printing number	update
1	2	Formerly *LEED NC Solved Problems: New Construction*.
1	3	Minor corrections.
1	4	Minor corrections.

PPI
1250 Fifth Avenue, Belmont, CA 94002
(650) 593-9119
www.ppi2pass.com

ISBN-13: 978-1-59126-118-6
ISBN-10: 1-59126-118-X

Table of Contents

Preface and Acknowledgments

Our desire to play a larger role in influencing the performance of buildings and their impact on the environment has led to our work at Be Green Consulting™ (BGC). In addition to consulting in sustainable design oriented to providing a healthy and productive environment for occupants, BGC also provides educational services in green building and LEED®* certification processes through workshops and presentations.

The growing importance of LEED accreditation was our catalyst to work with PPI on *LEED NC Practice Problems*, the first solved problems book published for this emerging field. This book was created to help individuals become LEED Accredited Professionals by providing problems that evaluate one's knowledge of green building strategies and technologies and enhance one's ability to relate these strategies and technologies to the LEED Green Building Rating System. There is no better way to evaluate one's green building and LEED knowledge than by applying these strategies to realistic project scenarios.

Though the project scenarios, vicinity plans, illustrations, practice problems and solutions presented in this book are realistic, they are all original, hypothetical situations based on what we have encountered in our design work and teaching.

We wish to acknowledge those who have helped us in the creation of this book, including Timothy Moore, Integrated Sustainable Design Consultant, LEED AP, who technically reviewed and provided insightful comments on our draft manuscript, and the PPI staff who saw the editorial and production work through to the end: project editor Jenny Lindeburg; typesetter, illustrator, and cover designer Amy Schwertman; editorial director Sarah Hubbard; and production director Cathy Schrott.

Meghan Peot, MEd
Brennan Schumacher, LEED AP

Introduction

About This Book

LEED NC Practice Problems prepares you for the Leadership in Energy and Environmental Design (LEED) Professional Accreditation exam given by the U.S. Green Building Council (USGBC) in coordination with the Green Building Certification Institute (GBCI). The problems and solutions presented in this book are based on the LEED-NC Rating System version 2.2. They offer you the opportunity to develop a comprehensive understanding of the LEED-NC Rating System, and were designed to correspond to the LEED-NC Accreditation Exam's scenario-problem style questions.

About the LEED Professional Accreditation Exam

The LEED Rating System is a voluntary, consensus-based national standard for developing high-performance, sustainable buildings. Members of the USGBC, representing all segments of the building industry, developed LEED and continue to contribute to its evolution.

Buildings become LEED certified, but individuals become LEED accredited. As defined by the USGBC and the Green Building Certification Institute in their publication *LEED Accredited Professional Candidate Handbook*, the LEED-NC Professional Accreditation exam is designed to ensure that a successful candidate has the knowledge and skills necessary to participate in the design process, to support and encourage integrated design, and to streamline a building project's LEED application and certification process. Exam questions are designed to test your understanding of green building practices and principles and familiarity with LEED requirements, resources, and processes. Exam questions are based on the LEED-NC Rating System and *Reference Guide*, which are used in the certification process for new construction.

The exam tests for minimum competency in four subject areas of the LEED certification process. These are identified by USGBC as follows.

- Knowledge of LEED Credit Intents and Requirements
- Coordinate Project and Team

- Implement LEED Process
- Verify, Participate in, and Perform Technical Analyses Required for LEED Credits

Each subject area is weighted to reflect its relative importance to the practice of a LEED Accredited Professional. These subject areas and their weighting are based on studies known as "task analyses" or "job analyses," which identify the knowledge, skills, and abilities needed of LEED Accredited Professionals working on LEED projects.

The exam is comprised of 80 randomly delivered multiple-choice questions that must be completed in 2 hours. Each question has four or more options to choose from. In some cases more than one option is correct, and the examinee must select all correct options to correctly answer the question. To ensure that your chances of passing remain constant regardless of the particular administration of the exam taken, the USGBC converts the raw exam score to a scaled score, with the total number of points set at 200 and a minimum passing score of 170. In other words, you are not penalized if the exam taken is more difficult than usual. Instead, fewer questions must be answered correctly to achieve a passing score.

The LEED Professional Accreditation exam currently offers three exam tracks: LEED for New Construction (LEED-NC), LEED for Commercial Interiors (LEED-CI), and LEED for Existing Buildings (LEED-EB). Each exam track is based on a specific version of the respective LEED Rating System and you must choose one of these tracks to be tested under. Any one of these tracks will provide you with the LEED AP credential, which is applicable to all LEED Rating Systems.

Taking the Exam

The exam is administered by computer at any Prometric test site. Thomson Prometric is a third party testing agency with over 250 testing locations in the United States. When scheduling an exam, you must first register at www.gbci.org. Then you must go to the Prometric website at www.prometric.com/usgbc to schedule and pay for the exam. All cancellations and rescheduling must be done directly with Prometric. GBCI recommends that you show up a half hour before your exam appointment to check in and get settled.

You don't need much experience with computers to take the exam. A 15-minute tutorial is available for you to take before beginning the actual exam. Questions and answer choices are shown on a computer screen, and the computer keeps track of which answers you choose. You can skip questions, mark questions to look at later, and change your answers as often as time permits.

While taking the exam, it's better to never leave a question unanswered, even if it's one you want to skip and come back to. Instead, make your best, quick guess right away and mark the question to look at again later. If you decide on a different answer later, you can change it, but if you run out of time before getting to all your skipped questions, you will still have guessed at each one.

Upon completing the exam, you will immediately receive your score. There is a 15-minute exit survey which completes the 2 hour and 30 minute exam experience. When exiting the examination room, an exam attendant will distribute your LEED Professional Accreditation Exam Score Report. If you pass, a LEED AP Certificate will follow in the mail.

How to Use This Book

To do well on the real exam, you'll need two things: knowledge of the LEED-NC Rating System and the ability to bring up that knowledge under time pressure. The *LEED NC Practice Problems* will help you improve both.

You should first complete the general LEED problems before progressing to the project scenarios. These general problems are designed to gage your basic comprehension of the LEED Rating System and *Reference Guide.* Upon completion of the problems, check the solutions to see if there are specific areas or topics that require further study.

It is recommended that you complete one project scenario at a time. Each project contains a vicinity plan, a scenario, an informational table, and multiple questions that are drawn from the following six LEED-NC Rating System categories.

- sustainable sites (SS)
- water efficiency (WE)
- energy and atmosphere (EA)
- materials and resources (MR)
- indoor environmental quality (EQ)
- innovation and design process (ID)

Carefully read the project scenario and look over its informational table and vicinity plan to get a feel for the scope and program of the project. Read each question and reference the project scenario information.

Complete each question using the LEED-NC Rating System version 2.2, the *LEED-NC Reference Guide version 2.2*, the USGBC website, and any other appropriate internet resources. Once you feel you have correctly and completely answered each question, check your answers by referring to the solutions provided at the end of each chapter. Notice your areas of strength and weakness.

Note that the book's Innovation and Design Process problems and solutions are based on hypothetical project scenarios. Some of the answers were derived from researching past Innovation in Design Credit Interpretation Rulings. The authors have not formally submitted the suggested innovations to the USGBC for approval. Therefore, if pursuing any of the innovations, it would be wise to research current Innovation in Design Credit Interpretation Rulings, or submit Credit Interpretation Requests to the USGBC.

LEED NC Practice Problems does not mimic the exact format of the LEED-NC Accreditation exam. However, its problems and solutions provide an opportunity for you to assess your knowledge of green building strategies within the context of the LEED-NC Rating System, and allow you to practice your problem solving skills.

General LEED Problems

1. What is a synergy (as it relates to the LEED-NC Rating System)?

2. What is a trade-off (as it relates to the LEED-NC Rating System)?

3. How do you register a project for LEED certification?

4. USGBC allows project teams to submit documentation for LEED project certification in either of two phases. What are these two phases?

5. What is the difference between LEED certification and LEED accreditation? Describe these two processes.

6. Can a product be LEED certified?

7. There are two types of Innovation in Design (ID) credits in the LEED-NC Rating System. Name and describe them.

8. What does CIR stand for? What is a CIR? Where/how do you find them?

9. What resources does the USGBC make available through their website?

10. What are the categories of project costs for LEED certification?

General LEED Solutions

1. A synergy, as it relates to the LEED-NC Rating System, is a green building strategy that contributes to the achievement of more than one LEED credit. Recognizing opportunities to apply synergistic green building strategies is the result of a successful design process that integrates building systems and elicits input from all team members.

    For example, a project that includes a vegetated roof (also known as a green roof) in its design can use the following synergy opportunities to achieve more than one LEED credit.

    *   SS Credit 6.1, Stormwater Design: Quantity Control requires a project to limit the disruption of a site's natural hydrology by managing the amount of stormwater runoff. A vegetated roof can help manage stormwater runoff by increasing the area of permeable surfaces and allowing for more on-site infiltration.

    *   SS Credit 6.2, Stormwater Design: Quality Control requires a project to limit the disruption and pollution of natural water flows by managing stormwater runoff. A vegetated roof limits such disruption and pollution and improves the quality of stormwater runoff by filtering out and decreasing the amount of pollutants from the rainwater.

    *   SS Credit 7.2, Heat Island: Roof requires a project to reduce the heat island effect (the phenomenon whereby an urban or suburban area has significantly higher air temperatures than its rural surroundings) in order to minimize negative impacts on human and wildlife habitats. A vegetated roof can reduce the heat island effect by reducing the surface area of heat-absorbing roofing materials, such as asphalt, and replacing these materials with various types of vegetative ground covers and grasses.

    *   EA Credit 1, Optimize Energy Performance requires a project to improve energy performance above the baseline by employing energy efficient strategies and equipment selections. In most cases, a vegetated roof has a higher insulation value than most energy codes require, and can improve energy performance above the required baseline.

2. A trade-off, as it relates to the LEED-NC Rating System, is a relationship between green building strategies that has an adverse effect on the achievement of more than one LEED credit. The project team must weigh the benefits and costs of each of the conflicting green building strategies and present them to the owner. The decision of which strategy to implement is ultimately based on the owner's priorities. Recognizing these trade-offs is part of a successful design process that integrates building systems and elicits input from all team members.

For example, achieving EQ Credit 2, Increased Ventilation, provides building occupants with more fresh air than is required by codes. However, in mechanical systems the additional fresh air brought into the building needs conditioning, which uses energy. If occupant comfort and energy efficiency cannot both be successfully obtained, the project team and owner must decide which credit is the higher priority.

3. To register a project for LEED certification, the project team's administrator must:

1. Attain the LEED Project Registration form from www.usgbc.org under the LEED portion of the website.

2. Complete and submit the registration form online by supplying the following.
   a. the project type
   b. general project information
   c. primary contact information
   d. project owner information
   e. project details
   f. payment information

Once the registration form is submitted, USGBC sends a confirmation email that includes the LEED Project Access ID number. This ID number allows project administrators and team members to access LEED-Online, an electronic interface that allows project teams to submit 100% of their documentation online for LEED project certification.

4. The design phase and the construction phase are the two phases in which project teams may submit documentation for LEED-NC project certification.

5. The difference between LEED accreditation and LEED certification is that people are accredited and buildings are certified.

The LEED Professional Accreditation exams are designed to ensure that a successful candidate has the knowledge and skills necessary to participate in the design process, to support and encourage integrated design, and to streamline a building project's LEED registration and certification process. Other than passing the LEED Professional Accreditation exam, there are no prerequisites for becoming a LEED AP.

To achieve LEED certification, a project must be eligible for one of the USGBC certification tracks, be registered with the USGBC, satisfy all the LEED Rating System prerequisites, and achieve a minimum number of points. The LEED rating level (Certified, Silver, Gold, or Platinum) awarded to a project is dependent on the points earned. Once a project is registered, the certification process may begin. The following phases are included in the LEED certification process.

- *application and documentation submittals*: A project team may submit their application and documentation by using LEED-Online.

- *LEED technical reviews*: A project team's submitted credits are reviewed.

- *certification award*: If a project passes certification, the USGBC presents the team with an award letter, certificate, and metal LEED plaque indicating the certification level.

- *appeal*: A project team may appeal a credit denied in the Final LEED Review if it feels sufficient grounds to do so exist.

For more information about the LEED certification process, go to the USGBC website at www.usgbc.org.

6. Products cannot be LEED certified. While a product can contribute to the achievement of a certain LEED credit, the product is never certified on its own accord.

7. The LEED-NC Rating System's innovation and design process provides project teams the opportunity to be awarded points for exemplary performance above the set requirements of the LEED-NC Rating System, and/or for innovative strategies in building categories not specifically addressed by the LEED-NC Rating System. There are two categories of Innovation in Design (ID) credits a project team may achieve. They include:

- *exemplary performance*: ID credits for exemplary performance are generally awarded for doubling the credit requirements and/or achieving the next incremental percentage threshold.

- *innovative strategies*: ID credits for innovative strategies are awarded for comprehensive strategies that demonstrate significant and quantifiable environmental and/or health benefits.

8. CIR stands for both Credit Interpretation Request and Credit Interpretation Ruling. Typically, a project team would submit a Credit Interpretation Request to the USGBC when there are problems or questions about meeting a credit's requirements. The USGBC answers these requests with a Credit Interpretation Ruling. These rulings set the precedent for future projects and can be used as a reference. A list of CIRs can be found on the USGBC website (www.usgbc.org), and on the LEED-Online website (http://leedonline.usgbc.org).

9. The USGBC offers the following resources through their website (www.usgbc.org):
- LEED Rating Systems
- LEED Reference Guides
- brochures and FAQs
- case studies
- PowerPoint® presentations
- credit templates
- web-based learning
- research
- publications

- green building links
- credit interpretation rulings (CIRs)
- *LEED Professional Accreditation Exam Candidate Handbook*
- web-login access

10. The fee categories for LEED certification are registration, design submittal, and construction submittal. The registration fees are fixed rate. The design submittal and construction submittal fees are based on the square footage of the project. USGBC members recieve discounts on all three fees. There are additional fees for LEED Review Appeals Credit Interpretation Requests.

Environmental Learning Center Problems

1

Vicinity Plan

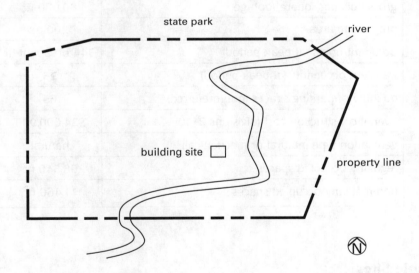

building site

state park

river

property line

N

Scenario

Good View is a rural community in central Colorado at 9000 ft above sea level. A non-profit institute plans to construct a new environmental learning center on a previously impacted site in Good View. The site is adjacent to a state park, and the learning center will be maintained and operated by a full-time staff. The facility will serve as an educational center for the general public and local schools. It will also cater to the professional needs of geologists, wildlife biologists, botanists, and astronomers. The facility will serve as the headquarters for a research team studying the decreasing local lynx population, which is federally threatened and state endangered. Biologists will study the facility's fully functional Living Machine® (a bioremediation wastewater treatment system) to see how it performs at high altitudes. Local astronomers will use the facility's new high-powered telescope for research and educational classes.

The facility will be naturally ventilated and will be constructed using fire-retardant, high-performance insulated concrete forms (ICF) that are manufactured locally. It will also be off-grid (not connected to a utility transmission or distribution system) and powered by photovoltaics (PVs) and three on-site wind turbines. The building project team will work with a daylighting lab to effectively use daylight to decrease the need for electric lighting in the building. Additionally, this project team will take great care not to disturb the natural areas surrounding the facility. The team will extensively restore the site's vegetation with native plants, as the ecosystem is a habitat for a diverse selection of flora and fauna. Furthermore, there will be no irrigation systems installed. To demonstrate their commitment to the environment, the owners have requested the facility design be low maintenance and practical.

General Information	
project building footprint	55,000 ft^2
gross building square footage	80,000 ft^2
project site area	200 ac
occupant hours (at peak period)	344 occupant-hr
transient occupants (at peak period)	25
quantity of parking spaces (non-preferred)	65
overall construction cost (divisions 2–10)	$24,000,000
ventilation type (natural or mechanical)	natural
regularly occupied spaces	68,540 ft^2
non-regularly occupied spaces	11,460 ft^2

Sustainable Sites

1. The project design team will use soil stabilization and structural control measures to comply with the requirements of SS Prerequisite 1, Construction Activity Pollution Prevention. Specify three stabilization control technologies and four structural control technologies. Keeping in mind the project's goals and limitations, explain which technologies are most appropriate for the project.

2. Will this project meet the requirements of SS Credit 1, Site Selection? If yes, what must be submitted? If no, explain why not.

3. The environmental learning center will coordinate with schools to provide transportation for students visiting the center. Does this coordination meet the criteria for SS Credit 4.1, Alternative Transportation: Public Transportation Access?

4. The design team has sized the facility's parking capacity to meet the requirements of SS Credit 4.4: Alternative Transportation: Parking Capacity, Option 1. How many preferred parking spaces for carpools or vanpools must be provided?

5. The site for the environmental learning center is a greenfield that is adjacent to a state park. The owners and all stakeholders in the project are concerned with the negative impact the development of the site could have on the ecosystem. The project team has made these concerns the primary focus of the construction phase and would like to take all necessary steps to mitigate the risk of habitat loss. What credit will ensure the protection of the greenfield? What is required for documentation of this credit?

6. The project team is committed to the preservation of the lynx habitat and has minimized the development footprint as much as possible. They expect to receive one point for SS Credit 5.2, Site Development: Maximize Open Space. The open space required by zoning in Good View for this type of project is 25% of the site excluding the building footprint. What is the total amount of open space required for the project to receive one point for SS Credit 5.2?

7. Using the following measurements, complete the calculations required for documentation of SS Credit 7.2, Heat Island Effect: Roof.

   - roof surface area: 55,000 ft^2
   - PV panels: 10,000 ft^2
   - white EPDM (ethylene, propylene, diene monomer) material: SRI of 84; 40,000 ft^2
   - red clay tile: SRI of 36; 5000 ft^2
   - low-sloped roof

8. The project owners have indicated that the lighting must be considerate of the astronomers' activities. Since the facility includes a telescope, on-site light pollution must be kept to a minimum. The LEED-NC Rating System uses SS Credit 8, Light Pollution Reduction, to address exterior lighting conditions. The electrical engineer has indicated to the project's LEED AP that all luminaires will meet the cutoff classification of the Illuminating Engineering Society of North America (IESNA). Why is the use of cutoff luminaires not compliant with LEED standards for this project, and to which referenced standard should the LEED AP refer the electrical engineer?

Water Efficiency

9. How does a Living Machine or wastewater aquatic system relate to water efficiency? Which credit does this strategy apply to? How does it apply?

10. What green building strategies could the environmental learning center employ to achieve WE Credit 3, Water Use Reduction?

11. Using the following data, calculate the project's percentage of water use reduction and determine which credits are achieved.

- baseline case total daily volume: 1350 gal

- design case total daily volume: 720 gal

- annual work days: 350 days

- rainwater volume: 0 gal/yr   (0 gal/day)

Energy and Atmosphere

12. What systems must be commissioned according to EA Prerequisite 1, Fundamental Commissioning of the Building Energy Systems?

13. The environmental learning center is an off-grid facility that must operate in the most energy efficient manner in order to minimize the amount of power required on site. How can the regulated building systems as defined by ASHRAE 90.1-2004 be addressed to decrease energy consumption?

14. The project may incorporate on-site renewable energy systems which will help earn points under EA Credit 1, Optimize Energy Performance. Describe the process that must be completed to document energy performance for the off-grid facility to receive maximum points for this EA credit.

15. The project scenario discusses two methods for creating renewable energy through photovoltaics (PVs) and wind turbines. What other renewable energy systems might this project use to provide energy to the building?

16. The environmental learning center is an off-grid facility that must harvest as much "free" energy as possible to reduce the amount of power needed from the on-site photovoltaics and wind turbines. What strategies can be implemented to harvest natural resources on site?

17. The project is considering EA Credit 5, Measurement and Verification. The owners are concerned with additional costs for LEED certification and have asked what factors affect the cost and accuracy of this credit. Explain these factors.

Materials and Resources

18. According to the recycling area guidelines in the *LEED-NC Reference Guide*, what is the minimum recycling area necessary for the project to meet MR Prerequisite 1, Storage and Collection of Recyclables?

19. The general contractor has begun to set up calculations for MR Credits 3–6. The LEED-NC Rating System provides two options for determining the total materials cost for the project. Explain and include the advantages and the disadvantages of each option.

20. The general contractor has submitted documentation that confirms the rebar to be used on the project contains recycled content. The LEED AP on the job requests that the contractor confirm whether this is pre-consumer or post-consumer recycled content. What is the difference between pre-consumer and post-consumer recycled content? How does the type of recycled content impact the value used to document MR Credit 4, Recycled Content?

21. The general contractor has submitted acoustical tile containing recycled content to contribute to MR Credit 4, Recycled Content. Based on the following information, what is the recycled content value of the acoustical tile?

- total cost of construction (divisions 2–10): $24,000,000

- total cost of installed material (divisions 2–10): $10,800,000

- total cost of acoustical tile (material only): $12,300

- recycled content of acoustical tile: 40% pre-consumer; 60% post-consumer

22. The project design team is striving to earn one point for MR Credit 5, Regional Materials. Based on the 45% default materials value, what is the minimum dollar amount of regional materials necessary to earn this point?

23. The contractor has determined that only a portion of the components used in some assemblies were extracted from within a 500 mi radius. Explain how assemblies containing components from both inside and outside a 500 mi project radius provide value in MR Credit 5, Regional Materials.

24. The general contractor has indicated that in order to achieve MR Credit 7, Certified Wood, the project should apply the following strategies.

a. The general contractor will utilize reused wood for concrete forming.

b. The general contractor will use FSC certified wood for dimensional lumber and finished and rough carpentry.

c. All wood purchased for bracing will be virgin, non-FSC certified wood, but will be reused on future projects.

d. The project will use salvaged wood flooring from a local high school gym for hardwood floors in conference rooms.

e. All wood provided by the owner will not be FSC certified wood, but will be urea-formaldehyde free.

Explain which of these products will help contribute to the goal of using 50% FSC certified wood to achieve MR Credit 7.

Indoor Environmental Quality

25. List three methods of natural ventilation as determined by ASHRAE 62.1-2004. What is required to document compliance with EQ Prerequisite 1, Minimum IAQ Performance?

26. Describe the documentaion requirements the environmental learning center must meet for EQ Credit 1, Outdoor Air Delivery Monitoring.

27. EQ Credit 3.2, Construction IAQ Management Plan: Before Occupancy, Option 2, requires that the indoor air of a building be tested for which contaminants? Why is testing for contaminants important?

28. The project team is documenting compliance with EQ Credit 4.2, Low-Emitting Materials: Paints and Coatings. What must be submitted to USGBC to document compliance?

29. The owners of the project have determined that they would like to eliminate all added urea-formaldehyde from composite woods and agrifiber products in order to achieve EQ Credit 4.4, Low-Emitting Materials: Composite Wood and Agrifiber Products. What is urea-formaldehyde and why is it important to eliminate it from indoor environments?

30. During the project's construction phase, the owners realized they wanted to comply with EQ Credit 5, Indoor Chemical and Pollutant Source Control. Since the project is under construction and cannot use permanently installed grates, grilles, or slotted systems, how can the project team achieve a point for EQ Credit 5?

31. The project team is designing a natural ventilation system to cool and vent the building. ASHRAE 55-2004 provides an optional method for naturally ventilated spaces, which USGBC references for compliance with EQ Credit 7.1, Thermal Comfort: Design. How does this approach account for the additional variables presented with natural systems?

32. In order to properly document EQ Credit 7.2, Thermal Comfort: Verification, what corrections should the LEED AP note in the following narrative prior to submitting it to the USGBC?

> *The owners of the environmental learning center will conduct a survey of all visitors 24 months after occupancy. Corrections and adjustments will be made to the HVAC systems where surveys indicate problems in comfort for more than 25% of the visitors. The owners will use ASHRAE 55-2004 as a reference standard for environmental variables in potential problem areas.*

33. The project team will be working with a daylighting lab. They will use a physical model to analyze shading techniques. They will also use this model for comparing daylighting strategies, but the model will not provide the same results as a daylight simulation model for documentation of EQ Credit 8.1, Daylight and Views: Daylight 75% of Spaces. Without paying a consultant to run a daylighting simulation model, describe how this project can still earn a point for EQ Credit 8.1.

Innovation and Design Process

34. One of the biologists employed by the environmental learning center is a LEED Accredited Professional (AP) and sat in on a design charette. Does the biologist's attendance to one design charette meet the criteria for ID Credit 2, LEED Accredited Professional? What are the submittal requirements for ID Credit 2?

35. List two potential exemplary performance strategies based on the project scenario. Explain how each meets requirements for ID Credit 1, Innovation in Design for Exemplary Performance.

36. List two potential innovative performance strategies based on the project scenario. Explain how each meets requirements for ID Credit 1, Innovation in Design.

Environmental Learning Center Solutions

Sustainable Sites

1. Soil stabilization control technologies include:

   - *temporary seeding*: using fast-growing vegetative cover for short-term (less than one year) control on disturbed areas that may be in danger of erosion

   - *permanent seeding*: establishing grass, trees, and shrubs for long-term control of soil erosion and permanent stabilization of the soil; unlike temporary seeding, permanent seeding requires that the construction phase be complete

   - *mulching*: covering soil with hay, grass, woodchips, straw, or gravel to hold soil in place and aid vegetation growth

   Structural control technologies include:

   - *earth dike*: a temporary berm, mound, or ridge of stabilized soil to divert surface runoff volumes from disturbed areas in order to channel water into sediment basins or sediment traps

   - *silt fence*: a fence or barrier with a filter fabric media to intercept runoff and trap/retain sediment from stormwater volumes flowing through the fence

   - *sediment trap*: a pond area or constructed earthen embankment designed to collect soil material transported in runoff and to mitigate siltation of natural drainage features

   - *sediment basin*: a pond with a controlled water release structure designed to hold stormwater for a period of time to allow sediment and other suspended material to settle from stormwater volumes

   The project design team wants to minimize the impact the development will have on the local environment. Soil stabilization control technologies such as temporary and permanent seeding and mulching will have a much lower environmental impact than most structural control measures, with the exception of a silt fence. The civil engineer will make the final decision on what technologies are employed on the project based on United States EPA Document No. EPA 832R92005, or based on a more stringent local code. The civil engineer will work with the local authority and the general contractor to meet local codes and to meet the owner's requests when the requests are possible.

2. This project will not meet the requirements to earn SS Credit 1, Site Selection. To meet the requirements, a project development cannot use land that is specifically identified as a habitat for federal or state threatened, and/or endangered, species. The project scenario states that the site is home to a decreasing local lynx population, which is both a federally threatened and state endangered species. While the project team could submit a Credit Interpretation Request (CIR) to the USGBC arguing that the lynx population will actually benefit from the research conducted at the learning center, ultimately, once the project is complete the learning center will attract more visitors to the site and the increased foot traffic will negatively impact the lynx's habitat. Therefore, this project will not meet the requirements of SS Credit 1.

(Note: To search the U.S. Fish and Wildlife Service's Threatened and Endangered Species database System (TESS), which daily provides an updated report of all listed species, go to www.fws.gov/endangered/wildlife.html. For more information about endangered species, go to the U.S. Fish and Wildlife Service's website, www.fws.gov/endangered.)

3. Coordinating transportation between the learning center and the local schools does not meet the criteria for SS Credit 4.1, Alternative Transportation: Public Transportation Access. This credit requires a facility to provide regularly scheduled public transportation. Coordinated transportation between the center and schools is considered chartered transportation and does not qualify according the LEED-NC Rating System.

4. SS Credit 4.4, Alternative Transportation: Parking Capacity, Option 1, requires a project's parking capacity to meet, but not exceed, minimum local zoning requirements, and to provide preferred parking for carpools or vanpools for 5% of the total provided parking spaces.

There are 65 parking spaces included in the design of the project. To calculate the number of required preferred parking spaces, multiply the total number of spaces by 5%.

$$\text{preferred parking spaces} = (65 \text{ spaces})(0.05)$$
$$= 3.25 \text{ spaces} \quad (4 \text{ spaces})$$

The project must provide 4 preferred parking spaces to receive a point for SS Credit 4.4, Alternative Transportation: Parking Capacity.

5. SS Credit 5.1, Site Development: Protect or Restore Habitat, Option 1 refers to the protection of the greenfield. To achieve this credit, the project team must document that it has limited all site disturbances to

- 40 ft beyond a building's perimeter
- 10 ft beyond surface walkways, patios, surface parking, and utilities less than 12 in in diameter
- 15 ft beyond primary roadway curbs and main utility branch trenches
- 25 ft beyond constructed areas with permeable surfaces that require additional staging areas in order to limit compaction in constructed areas

6. In order to receive a point for SS Credit 5.2, Site Development: Maximize Open Space, the team must meet the requirements Option 1. The vegetated open space within the project's boundary must exceed the local zoning's open space requirement for the site by 25%. To determine the total amount of open space required, use the following information.

- building footprint: $55{,}000 \text{ ft}^2$
- project site area: $(200 \text{ ac})\left(43{,}560 \dfrac{\text{ft}^2}{\text{ac}}\right) = 8{,}712{,}000 \text{ ft}^2$
- site excluding the building footprint: $8{,}712{,}000 \text{ ft}^2 - 55{,}000 \text{ ft}^2 = 8{,}657{,}000 \text{ ft}^2$
- open space required by zoning: $(8{,}657{,}000 \text{ ft}^2)(0.25) = 2{,}164{,}250 \text{ ft}^2$

Then, calculate the total open space required. (Note: the open space required by zoning must be converted from square feet to acres.)

$$\text{total open space required} = (\text{open space required by zoning})(1.25)$$

$$= (2{,}164{,}250 \text{ ft}^2)(1.25)\left(2.29 \times 10^{-5} \dfrac{\text{ac}}{\text{ft}^2}\right)$$

$$= (2{,}705{,}312.5 \text{ ft}^2)\left(2.29 \times 10^{-5} \dfrac{\text{ac}}{\text{ft}^2}\right)$$

$$= 62.1 \text{ ac}$$

7. To complete the calculations required for documentation of SS Credit 7.2, Heat Island Effect: Roof, the appropriate option must first be determined. Since this project does not have plans to include a vegetated roof, choose option 1. Option 1 requires the use of roofing materials that have a solar reflectance index (SRI) equal to or greater than the values in the following table for a minimum of 75% of the roof surface.

roof type	slope	SRI
low-sloped roof	≤ 2:12	78
steep-sloped roof	> 2:12	29

step 1: Calculate total roof surface area. Deduct areas with equipment, solar energy panels, and appurtenances.

$$\text{total roof surface area} = 55{,}000 \text{ ft}^2 - 10{,}000 \text{ ft}^2 \text{ of PV panels}$$

$$= 45{,}000 \text{ ft}^2$$

step 2: Determine if the roof surface area meets the applicable SRI criteria. The problem statement indicated that the project has a low-sloped roof, so materials used must have an SRI greater than or equal to 78. The environmental learning center is using white EPDM (ethylene, propylene, diene monomer) and a red clay tile. The red clay tile has an SRI of 36 which does not meet SRI requirements for a low-sloped roof; however, the white EPDM has an SRI of 84, which does meet the SRI requirements.

step 3: Determine if the qualified roof surface area meets the credit requirement by using Eq. 1 found in the *LEED-NC Reference Guide*. The following equation uses weighted averages in order to determine if the qualified roof area is greater than or equal to the total roof area.

Equation 1:

$$\frac{\text{area of SRI roof}}{0.75} + \frac{\text{area of vegetated roof}}{0.5} \geq \text{total roof area}$$

$$\frac{40{,}000 \text{ ft}^2}{0.75} + \frac{0 \text{ ft}^2}{0.5} \geq 45{,}000 \text{ ft}^2$$

$$\frac{40{,}000 \text{ ft}^2}{0.75} + 0 \text{ ft}^2 = 53{,}333 \text{ ft}^2$$

Since 53,333 sq ft is greater than 45,000 sq ft, the project does meet the requirements of Option 1, SS Credit 7.2, Heat Island Effect: Roof.

8. The LEED AP should refer the electrical engineer to the Illuminating Engineer Society of North America (IESNA) *Recommended Practice Manual: Lighting for Exterior Environments* (RP-33-99). SS Credit 8, Light Pollution Reduction references IESNA RP-33-99. This standard establishes four lighting zones (LZs) that dictate the lighting requirements a project must fulfill. Because the environmental learning center is in a rural setting, it is classified under lighting zone 1 (LZ1): dark. Therefore, in accordance with LZ1, all of the project's exterior lighting must be classified as *full* cutoff luminaires. The use of cutoff luminaires as indicated by the electrical engineer will not be acceptable.

Water Efficiency

9. Using a Living Machine or wastewater aquatic system is a bioremediation wastewater treatment strategy that when located on site, applies to WE Credit 2, Innovative Wastewater Technologies. These strategies use localized natural treatment processes, such as microorganisms, fungi, green plants, or enzymes to treat the wastewater that is generated by the project site. Using these types of natural treatment processes minimizes or eliminates the impact of contaminants on the environment.

Implementing a Living Machine or wastewater aquatic system is related to water efficiency because the treated wastewater can be recycled and used for potable and non-potable water needs on site. Treating wastewater on site also reduces the strain on public infrastructures by reducing the use of energy, chemicals, and water.

10. Possible strategies the environmental learning center could employ to achieve WE Credit 3, Water Use Reduction, include low-flow water closets, low-flow and water-less urinals, composting toilets, low-flow showerheads, low-flow faucets, metered faucets, dual-flush water closets, and graywater systems.

11. The project's percentage of water use reduction can be determined using the following calculations.

design case total annual volume = (design case total daily volume − rainwater volume) × (total annual workdays)

$$= \left(720 \, \frac{gal}{day} - 0 \, \frac{gal}{day}\right)\left(350 \, \frac{day}{yr}\right)$$

$$= 252{,}000 \text{ gal/yr}$$

baseline case total annual volume = (baseline case total daily volume)(total annual workdays)

$$= \left(1350 \, \frac{gal}{day}\right)\left(350 \, \frac{day}{yr}\right)$$

$$= 472{,}500 \text{ gal/yr}$$

$$\% \text{ water use reduction} = (-1)\left(\frac{\text{design case total annual volume}}{\text{baseline case total annual volume}}\right)(100\%)$$

$$= (-1)\left(\frac{252{,}000 \, \frac{gal}{day}}{472{,}500 \, \frac{gal}{day}}\right)(100\%)$$

$$= 46.7\% \quad (47\%)$$

Three credits are achieved: WE Credit 3.1 and WE Credit 3.2, Water Use Reduction, as well as ID Credit 1, Exemplary Performance. The project's calculated 47% water use reduction meets the 20% and 30% requirements for WE Credit 3. It surpasses a projected water savings of 40%, which is necessary for ID Credit 1.

Energy and Atmosphere

12. Projects trying to achieve LEED certification are required to meet all LEED prerequisites. The following systems must be commissioned according to EA Prerequisite 1, Fundamental Commissioning of the Building Energy Systems.

- heating, ventilating, air conditioning, and refrigeration (HVAC&R) systems (mechanical and passive) and associated controls
- lighting and daylighting controls
- domestic hot water systems
- renewable energy systems (e.g., wind, solar, etc.)

13. To decrease energy consumption, the building envelope must be well insulated. Some alternative construction techniques that would meet this goal include structurally insulated panels and insulated concrete forms. The envelope should also be maximized for efficiency based on building orientation and exposure.

    Likewise, high-performance windows and glazing systems should be sized, specified, and located to maximize the efficiency of the building envelope, allowing controlled amounts of heat and light into the building at the most appropriate times of the day and year. High efficiency lighting and lighting controls, task lighting, and minimal site lighting will also decrease the energy consumption of the building.

    All mechanical systems must be appropriately sized, including HVAC&R and hot water systems. Hot water systems should include a boiler and/or hot water heaters with high efficiency ratings. All motors and permanent equipment should have high efficiency ratings and variable frequency drives where applicable. All systems should be designed according to occupant needs and schedule of occupancy. An integrated design approach will facilitate the effective functioning of these systems.

14. When a project incorporates on-site renewable energy systems or site recovered energy systems, it must provide a baseline design case modeled on a backup energy source, such as electricity or natural gas. The proposed building performance can be modeled and documented in one of two ways. If the building simulation program has the capability, model the systems directly in the proposed design energy model and document the results. If the building simulation program does not have the capability, model the systems using the exceptional calculation method and document the results.

15. Other renewable energy resources are solar thermal systems, bio-fuel based electrical systems, geothermal heating systems, geothermal electrical systems, and low impact hydroelectric systems. In coastal regions, an additional renewable energy resource would be wave and tidal power systems.

    Systems that are commonly mistaken for renewable energy systems that will not be acceptable to USGBC are passive solar strategies, architectural features, geoexchange systems, green power, and renewable energy from off-site resources.

16. To obtain a maximum amount of free energy, the environmental learning center could implement daylight harvesting techniques. Building orientation, shading devices, window glazing, and light shelves can help control and distribute daylight for interior spaces.

    The building can also take advantage of solar orientation by harvesting the thermal energy from the sun in the winter and protecting the building from solar gain through shading in the summer. This is accomplished by calculating the different angles of the sun at different times of day and different times of the year. The center can also implement natural ventilation. Windows can be located and controlled to take advantage of prevailing winds to help cool the building by moving air. Natural cooling can take place by opening the building to the cooler air at night. Thermal massing in specific areas can help to maximize these conditions.

Careful consideration must be given to the orientation and angle of the photovoltaics to maximize their contribution to the buildings energy supply. Likewise, the site must be studied to find the optimum locations for the wind turbines to take advantage of the strongest, most steady supplies of wind.

17. According to the *LEED-NC Reference Guide*, in general, higher measurement and verification intensity and rigor means higher project costs, both upfront and over time. The following is a list of factors that affect the cost and accuracy of EA Credit 5, Measurement and Verification.

  • level of detail and effort associated with verifying post-construction conditions

  • number and types of metering points

  • duration and accuracy of metering activities

  • number and complexity of dependent and independent variables that must be measured or determined on an ongoing basis

  • availability of existing data collecting systems

  • confidence and precision levels specified for analysis

Materials and Resources

18. Although there are no calculations required to demonstrate compliance with MR Prerequisite 1, Storage and Collection of Recyclables, USGBC does provide recycling guideline recommendations in the *LEED-NC Reference Guide*. The LEED-NC Rating System requires the project team to provide an easily accessible area dedicated to the collection and storage of recycling that is sized appropriately to the needs of building operations and building square footage. The recycling area guidelines state that 225 sq ft is the recommended minimum recycling area in order for the environmental learning center to meet MR Prerequisite 1. This is a slight revision from LEED-NC version 2.1, where square footage recommendations were not provided.

19. To determine the total materials cost for a project, the LEED-NC Rating System provides the following two options. The LEED-NC Rating System only looks at hard costs for materials in CSI Master Format 1995 Divisions 2–10.

Option 1: the total materials cost for divisions 2–10 is equal to 45% of the total construction cost for divisions 2–10

  Pro

  • The process of determining the total materials cost is fast and efficient.

  • It is easier to achieve credit requirements for projects with more than 45% materials costs.

  Con

  • It is harder to achieve credit requirements for projects with less than 45% materials costs.

Option 2: Compute actual materials costs for divisions 2–10 excluding all labor, overhead, profit, rental fees, etc.

Pro

- It is easier to achieve credit requirements for projects with less than 45% materials costs.

Con

- In some cases it is difficult and time consuming to deduce the materials costs from the labor and equipment costs for each material on the project.

- Some contractors may not be willing to share or divulge such information.

- It is harder to achieve credit requirements for projects with more than 45% materials costs.

20. According to the USGBC, pre-consumer material is defined as material diverted from the waste stream during the manufacturing process. Excluded is reutilization of materials such as rework, regrind, or scrap generated in a process and capable of being reclaimed within the same process that generated it. For example, waste plastic from the production of beverage bottles used to make carpeting is considered pre-consumer recycled content. However, waste plastic that is generated in the production of beverage bottles and then reused to again to make a beverage bottle is NOT pre-consumer material.

According to USGBC, post-consumer material is defined as waste material generated by households or by commercial, industrial facilities in their role as end-users of the product, and that can no longer be used for its intended purpose. Using the previous example, beverage bottles that have been used by the consumer and then recycled to be used in the production of carpet are considered post-consumer material.

The LEED-NC Rating System gives a weighted value to recycled content in MR Credit 4, Recycled Content. The full value of post-consumer recycled content is used in the calculations of MR Credit 4, while half of the value of pre-consumer recycled content is used in the calculations.

This is illustrated in the following equation.

recycled content value = (% post-consumer recycled content)(material cost)
    + (0.5)(% pre-consumer recycled content)
    × (material cost)

21. To determine the recycled content value of the acoustical tile, use the following information.

- total cost of construction (for divisions 2–10): $24,000,000

- total cost of installed material (for divisions 2–10): $10,800,000

- total cost of acoustical tile (material only): $12,300

- recycled content of acoustical tile: 40% pre-consumer; 60% post-consumer

recycled content value = (% post-consumer recycled content)(material cost) + (0.5)
    × (% pre-consumer recycled content)(material cost)

= (0.60)($12,300) + (0.5)(0.40)($12,300)

= $9840

22. The value of regional materials is calculated based on a percentage of the cost of regional materials to the overall materials costs of the project. The total value of materials used on the project can be provided by the general contractor based on actual costs, or it can be calculated as 45% of the construction costs for divisions 2–10. Actual costs of regional materials are for materials only and exclude the cost of labor, overhead, profit, and rental fees.

Based on the information provided in the project scenario, 45% of the construction cost is

$$(\$24,000,000)(0.45) = \$10,800,000$$

The percent value of regional materials is based on the following formula:

$$\% \text{ regional materials} = \frac{\text{cost of regional materials}}{\text{total materials cost}}$$

In order to earn one point in MR Credit 5, Regional Materials a minimum of 10% of the materials must be extracted, harvested, or recovered, as well as manufactured within 500 mi of the project site.

$$10\% \text{ regional materials} = \frac{\text{cost of regional materials}}{\$10,800,000}$$

$$\text{cost of regional materials} = (0.10)(\$10,800,000)$$

$$= \$1,080,000$$

The minimum value of regional materials necessary to earn MR Credit 5 is $1,080,000.

23. The *LEED-NC Reference Guide* defines assemblies as products that are composed of multiple materials, either in reaching a formulation for a material (i.e., composite wood panels), or of all the sub-components (i.e., window system). Assemblies are given recognition by the LEED-NC Rating System for the portion or percentage of the material (based on weight) that is extracted, processed, and manufactured within 500 mi of a project site. These percentages are used towards the achievement of MR Credit 5, Regional Materials.

24. Only one of the proposed strategies contribute to the project's goal of using 50% FSC certified wood to obtain one point for MR Credit 7, FSC Certified Wood.

a. *No*: The wood for concrete forming will be reused and is exempt from the wood cost calculations. Furthermore, the wood for concrete forming is not permanently installed on the project, and therefore will not contribute to the goal of using 50% FSC certified wood.

b. *Yes*: The project will use FSC certified wood for dimensional lumber and finished and rough carpentry. This will help contribute to the goal of using 50% FSC certified wood.

c. *No*: The wood for bracing is not permanently installed on the project, and therefore will not contribute to the goal of using 50% FSC certified wood.

d. *No*: Salvaged wood flooring from the local high school gym is reused and is exempt from these calculations.

e. *No*: If the wood materials provided by the owner are used as part of the project to earn EQ Credit 4.4, then it must be included in all materials and resource calculations. In this case, wood provided by the owner will not help contribute to FSC certified wood, but it will need to be included to remain consistent in materials and resource calculations.

Indoor Environmental Quality

25. ASHRAE 62.1-2004 states that natural ventilation can be provided by thermal, wind, or diffusion effects. Required documentation includes confirming that the project complies with ASHRAE 62.1-2004, Section 5.1, for the location and size of window openings. Additionally, the project team will need to provide project drawings to show naturally ventilated building zones and intentional openings.

26. Since the environmental learning center is a naturally ventilated building, EQ Credit 1, Outdoor Air Delivery Monitoring requires CO_2 monitors be located in the vertical breathing zone 3 ft to 6 ft above the floor. If the CO_2 monitors do not provide feedback to an automated building system, then the monitors must provide occupants with useful information about operational adjustments (e.g., opening or closing operable windows, turning fans on or off, or making manual adjustments to air dampers).

27. The indoor air of the building must be tested for concentration levels of formaldehyde, particulates (PM10), total volatile organic compounds (VOCs), 4-phenylcyclohexene (4-PCH), and carbon monoxide. It is important to test for these contaminants in order to reduce indoor air quality problems resulting from the construction process.

    During the energy crisis of the 1970s, some buildings were constructed without operable windows. This was a strategy to reduce energy consumption by creating a more airtight building. However, this limits the amount of fresh air in the buildings to the capacity of the mechanical systems, which can have a negative impact on the indoor air quality. Furthermore, indoor air quality decreases as a result of the chemicals introduced from cleaning supplies, the off-gassing of furniture, paints, adhesives and sealants, office equipment, and pesticides. Such chemicals can contribute to the causes of sick building syndrome (SBS) and building related illness (BRI). Symptoms of SBS and BRI include eye, ear, nose, throat, and skin irritations. Other health problems may also include allergic reactions and nausea that can cause discomfort and unnecessary absenteeism.

28. The project team must provide a list of each indoor paint and coating used on the project to be compliant with EQ Credit 4.2, Low-Emitting Materials: Paints and Coatings. The team must provide the manufacturer's name, the products' names, the specific volatile organic compound (VOC) data in units of grams per liter for each product, and the allowable VOC limit from the Green Seal Standard GS-11.

29. The Environmental Health Center, a division of the National Safety Council, describes formaldehyde as a colorless, strong-smelling gas. It is widely used to manufacture building materials and is an effective adhesive for laminating plywood and manufacturing particle board. Formaldehyde is a naturally occurring volatile organic compound (VOC) that is found in small amounts in animals and plants.

There are two types of formaldehyde resins: urea-formaldehyde (UF) and phenol formaldehyde (PF). Products made of urea-formaldehyde can release ("off-gas") formaldehyde gas at room temperatures, while products made of phenol formaldehyde generally emit lower levels of the gas. It is important to eliminate building products made with formaldehyde resins because formaldehyde is a carcinogen and, even at low levels, can have a harmful health effect on humans, including burning sensation in the eyes, nose and throat; nausea; coughing; chest tightness; wheezing; and skin rashes.

30. To ensure a point is earned for EQ Credit 5, Indoor Chemical and Pollutant Source Control in lieu of permanently installed entryway grates, grills, or slotted systems, the project team could provide roll-out mats at each regularly used entry point in the environmental learning center. However, these mats are only acceptable to USGBC when they are maintained on a weekly basis by a contracted service organization. Additionally, the project must meet other parameters specified for this credit not related to the entry ways.

31. ASHRAE 55-2004 recognizes that thermal responses differ in naturally ventilated spaces versus spaces that are mechanically conditioned. The alternative approach provided by ASHRAE offers a broader range of indoor operative temperatures as a function of mean monthly outdoor temperatures for thermal comfort while assuming light activity by occupants. In addition, the conditions are independent of humidity, air speed, and clothing considerations.

32. The LEED AP should note the following italicized corrections prior to submitting the narrative to the USGBC.

The owners of the environmental learning center will conduct a survey of *regular building occupants six to eighteen months* after occupancy. Corrections and adjustments will be made to the HVAC systems where surveys indicate problems in comfort for more than *20%* of the *regular building occupants*. The owners will use ASHRAE 55-2004 as a reference standard for environmental variables in potential problem areas.

33. To achieve EQ Credit 8.1, Daylight and Views: Daylight 75% of Spaces, a project has three options: calculate the glazing factor, perform a daylight simulation, or directly measure the daylight in a completed building. Since the environmental learning center is building a physical model and will not perform a daylight simulation, it may choose either EQ Credit 8.1 Option 1 or Option 3.

Option 1—Glazing Factor Calculation: Achieve a minimum glazing factor of 2% in a minimum of 75% of regularly occupied areas.

The *Illuminating Engineering Society of North America (IESNA) Lighting Handbook*, ninth edition, defines daylight factor as a measure of daylight illuminance at a point on a given plane, expressed as the ratio of the illuminance on the given plane at that point to the simultaneous exterior illuminance on a horizontal plane from the whole of an unobstructed sky of assumed or known luminance distribution. Direct sunlight is excluded from both interior and exterior values of illumination.

The *LEED-NC Reference Guide* uses a simplified version of this definition to define a glazing factor as the ratio of interior luminance at a given point on a given plane to the exterior illumination under known overcast sky conditions. Glazing factor is a proxy used by LEED in EQ Credit 8.1 methodology purposes. Note that the *LEED-NC Reference Guide* confuses the terms daylight factor and glazing factor.

Option 3—Daylight Measurement: Measure and confirm a minimum daylight illumination level of 25 footcandles has been achieved in at least 75% of regularly occupied areas. The *LEED-NC Reference Guide* states there are exceptions for areas where tasks would be hindered by the use of daylight and these areas will be considered on their merits.

Innovation and Design Process

34. The role of the biologist will not meet the criteria for ID Credit 2, LEED Accredited Professional (AP). In order to meet the criteria, at least one LEED AP must be a principal participant of the project team. The following must be submitted through the USGBC LEED-Online website.

- name of the LEED AP

- name of the LEED AP's company

- brief description of the LEED AP's project role(s)

- copy of the LEED AP certificate

Note: The following Innovation and Design Process solutions are based on hypothetical project scenarios and were derived from researching past Innovation in Design Credit Interpretation Rulings. These suggested innovations have not been formally submitted to the USGBC for approval. Therefore, if pursuing any of the following innovations, it is recommended one research current Innovation in Design Credit Interpretation Rulings, or submit Credit Interpretation Requests to the USGBC.

35. ID Credit 1, Innovation in Design for Exemplary Performance, provides design teams the opportunity to be awarded points for exceptional performance above the requirements set by the LEED-NC Rating System. Exemplary performance ID credits are generally awarded for doubling the credit requirements and/or achieving the next incremental percentage threshold. Based on the project scenario, the following options provide two potential opportunities to achieve ID Credit 1.

Option 1—SS Credit 5.1, Site Development: Protect or Restore Habitat—Exemplary Performance: The project scenario provided information indicating that an extensive restoration effort will take place to help minimize the impact on the local ecosystem. USGBC has set criteria for exemplary performance in SS Credit 5.1, Site Development, Protect or Restore Habitat, by protecting or restoring 75% of the site area with native or adaptive vegetation on previous developed or graded sites. This will exceed the base criteria set at 50%.

Option 2—EQ Credit 8.1, Daylight and Views: Daylight 75% of Spaces—Exemplary Performance: The project scenario indicates the project team will be working with a daylighting lab. Since the owner is a nonprofit, and the building is an off-grid facility, both cost- and energy-efficiency are of utmost importance. Maximizing daylighting will save energy and therefore reduce costs. A point will be received if the project can attain a 2% glazing factor in 95% of the regularly occupied areas. This will exceed the 2% glazing factor in 75% of the spaces as specified in EQ Credit 8.1.

36. ID Credit 1, Innovation in Design for Innovative Performance, provides design teams the opportunity to be awarded points for innovative performance outside of the requirements set by the LEED-NC Rating System. Innovative performance ID credits are generally awarded for comprehensive strategies that demonstrate significant and quantifiable environmental and/or health benefits. Based on the project scenario, the following options are two potential opportunities to achieve ID Credit 1.

Option 1—Public Education—Innovative Performance: The environmental learning center is an educational institution providing opportunities to visitors. In order to attain ID Credit 1, Innovation in Design, a comprehensive green building education program must exist. For example, educational signage and an interactive display, coupled with a website, video, and/or case study, are typically necessary and must be documented to achieve this credit.

Option 2—Net Zero Building—Exemplary Performance: The *LEED-NC Reference Guide* does provide an opportunity to achieve an exemplary performance ID credit for EA Credit 1. The environmental learning center is an off-grid facility in which 100% of the power will be created on site. This can be documented by modeling the energy systems directly in the proposed design energy simulation model or using the using the exceptional calculation method.

Downtown Office Building Problems

2

Vicinity Plan

project area

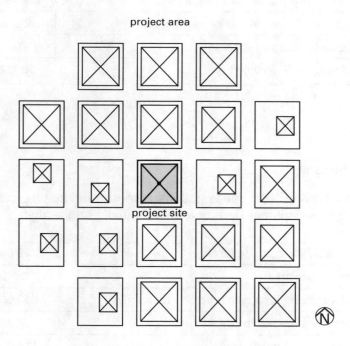

project site

Scenario

A single story, 13,235 sq ft warehouse in downtown San Franco, Oregon will be retrofitted and expanded. The building, which once housed chemicals, will become an office that is part of an urban industrial park. The redesign calls for 211,765 sq ft to be added to the original 13,235 sq ft. The new building will be a total of seventeen stories, with four floors available for rent to local small businesses and nonprofit organizations, and one floor dedicated to child care services. The owners will occupy the remaining above-grade floors and have requested independent controls for their employees wherever possible. The expansion also includes five floors of underground parking, which includes parking for adjacent building tenants.

To help control stormwater runoff and provide an open-air space for employees, vegetation will cover the majority of the roof. As the owners of the building are committed to green power, 100% of the building's power will be purchased from a Green-e certified source. Daylighting will be a primary focus of the building's new design, and to ensure its techniques are successfully integrated, the owners have asked the project team to collaborate with a local daylighting lab. Finally, the existing building's HVAC&R systems, which contain a chilled water system, will be reused.

General Information	
project building footprint	13,250 ft^2
gross building square footage	225,000 ft^2
project site area	0.38 ac
occupant hours (at peak period)	7032 occupant-hr
transient occupants (at peak period)	84
quantity of parking spaces	300
overall construction cost (divisions 2–10)	$78,750,000
ventilation type (natural or mechanical)	mechanical
regularly occupied spaces	168,750 ft^2
non-regularly occupied spaces	56,250 ft^2

Sustainable Sites

1. Given the following chart and equations, demonstrate the project's compliance with SS Credit 2, Development Density and Community Connectivity.

gross building square footage	225,000 ft^2
project site area	0.38 ac
total building area within density radius	850,000 ft^2
total site area within density radius	10.8 ac
undeveloped public areas, roads, right of ways within density radius	150,000 ft^2

$$\text{development density} = \frac{\text{gross building square footage}}{\text{project site area}}$$

$$\text{density radius} = 3\sqrt{\text{project site area}}$$

2. The owners believe the project site could be classified as a brownfield because the original building housed chemicals. The site is not currently classified as a brownfield. Who should the owners or project team seek out to classify the site as a brownfield in order to achieve SS Credit 3, Brownfield Redevelopment?

3. The building is located close to mass transit and public transportation. The owners would also like to promote the use of bicycles to reduce pollution. How many secure bicycle spaces and changing and showering facilities are required to meet SS Credit 4.2, Alternative Transportation: Bicycle Storage and Changing Rooms? Complete the following calculations.

   a. Find the number of full-time equivalent (FTE) occupants.

   b. Find the number of required secure bicycle spaces.

   c. Find the number of required changing and showering facilities.

4. The project design team is pursuing SS Credit 4.3, Alternative Transportation: Low-Emission and Fuel Efficient Vehicles via Option 2. How many preferred parking spaces must be provided?

5. The project design team is deciding which option to pursue for SS Credit 4.4, Alternative Transportation: Parking Capacity. Is SS Credit 4.4, Option 2 a viable choice? Why or why not?

6. The downtown office building is located in an urban area on a previously developed site. What green building strategy allows this project to achieve SS Credit 5.1, Site Development: Protect or Restore Habitat?

7. The project design team is discussing requirements for SS Credit 7.1, Heat Island Effect: Non-Roof. Based on the current design, which option is most appropriate for the design team to pursue? Why?

8. Based on the data in the project scenario, which option should the project team pursue in order to earn credit for SS Credit 7.2, Heat Island Effect: Roof? What are the requirements of this option?

Water Efficiency

9. The project team would like to achieve WE Credit 1.2, Water Efficient Landscaping: No Potable Water Use or No Irrigation. In order to make sure a permanent irrigation system is not necessary for the green roof, the team must carefully design and select vegetation. Decisions concerning the selection of vegetation will affect the landscape coefficient. Define the landscape coefficient and explain how it is calculated.

10. What standard does WE Credit 3, Water Use Reduction reference, and what will this referenced standard regulate relative to this project?

Energy and Atmosphere

11. What building components must meet ASHRAE/IESNA Standard 90.1-2004 to meet requirements for EA Prerequisite 2, Minimum Energy Performance?

12. The owners are expanding and retrofitting their existing building. What must the project team confirm and complete in order to comply with EA Prerequisite 3, Fundamental Refrigerant Management? What is its designated timeline for completion?

13. There are four options a project team may use to qualify for EA Credit 1, Optimize Energy Performance. Describe Option 1 and if it is applicable to this project.

14. In order to mitigate the potential for large utility bills due to the building's increased size and occupant load, the owners would like to reduce its energy consumption. Demand reduction is one strategy being pursued by the project team to reduce energy consumption at peak periods. Reducing the peak demands for energy will increase the point potential for EA Credit 1, Optimize Energy Performance. Explain how the design team can incorporate demand reduction into the project's design.

15. The project design team has used Option 1–Whole Building Energy Simulation, to achieve EA Credit 1, Optimize Energy Performance. The team is considering installing photovoltaics (PVs) on the building façade, integrating the PVs into the glazing systems, and using the PVs as shading devices. Describe how the performance rating method is used to calculate the percentage of on-site renewable energy to obtain EA Credit 2, On-site Renewable Energy.

16. The project team is comparing and contrasting the whole building energy simulation model and the environmental impact the building will have relative to global warming and ozone depletion. Describe the potential trade-off between EA Credit 1, Optimize Energy Performance and EA Credit 4, Enhanced Refrigerant Management.

17. The owners of the office building would like to purchase 100% of the building's electricity from a renewable energy resource. Describe the three approaches for achieving EA Credit 6, Green Power approved by the USGBC and specified in the LEED-NC Rating System.

Materials and Resources

18. The project team is in the process of determining which LEED Rating System will be most appropriate for this project. They have narrowed it down to LEED-EB and LEED-NC. What is the difference between LEED-NC and LEED-EB rating systems, and why would the project team choose the LEED-NC Rating System over the LEED-EB Rating System?

19. According to the requirements of MR Credit 1, Building Reuse, does the project qualify for this credit? Explain why or why not.

20. The square footage of the addition is over 200% of the existing building's square footage. The project will reuse interior materials, including steel studs, walls, doors, and casework. Which credit will this reuse strategy qualify for?

21. The general contractor would like to set up a spreadsheet to keep track of all the project's salvaged, refurbished, and reused materials. What material details are required for submittal documentation in order to achieve MR Credit 3, Materials Reuse?

22. The general contractor removed 136 tons of asphalt from the existing parking lot. The contractor plans to recycle and reuse this same asphalt for use at a different project site. Does recycling the asphalt in this manner meet the requirements of MR Credit 4, Recycled Content? Why or why not?

23. The design team is reusing as many materials as possible from the existing building. The lighting designer plans to reuse the building's existing doors by having them painted white and utilizing them as light shelves. These light shelves will be installed on the interior of the building and will help distribute and control the amount of daylight in the interior of the new building. Describe why reusing the existing doors will, or will not, apply to the following credits.

   a. MR Credit 1, Building Reuse

   b. MR Credit 2, Construction Waste Management

   c. MR Credit 3, Materials Reuse

   d. MR Credit 5, Regional Materials

   e. EA Credit 1, Optimize Energy Performance

   f. EQ Credit 8.1, Daylight and Views: Daylight 75% of Spaces

   g. EQ Credit 8.2, Daylight and Views: Views for 90% of Spaces

Indoor Environmental Quality

24. Describe how this project can meet the requirements of EQ Prerequisite 1, Minimum IAQ Performance.

25. The mechanical engineer for this project based the building's HVAC systems design on the following criteria.

   a. In all densely occupied spaces with an occupant density of at least 30 people per 1000 sq ft, the design calls for CO_2 concentration monitoring. CO_2 sensors shall be located in the vertical breathing zone, 3 ft to 6 ft above the floor.

   b. For each mechanical ventilation system in non-densely occupied spaces, the design calls for a measurement system that monitors the minimum outdoor airflow rate with an accuracy of plus or minus 20% of the design minimum outdoor air rate.

Do these criteria meet the parameters for EQ Credit 1, Outdoor Air Delivery Monitoring? Explain why or why not.

26. This project plans to install and use permanent air handlers during construction. What MERV value must the filtration media at each return air grille have in order to comply with EQ Credit 3.1, Construction IAQ Management Plan: During Construction? What does MERV stand for, and how does it relate to the indoor air quality (IAQ) during and after construction?

27. The office building owners have told the project design team that they want the office building to be fully operational and ready for occupancy as soon as possible. In response, the project team has decided to pursue EQ Credit 3.2, Construction IAQ Management Plan: Before Occupancy, Option 1–Flush-Out. The mechanical engineer has provided the LEED AP with the following plan.

   The owners have stated their desire to occupy the building at the earliest possible date. The owners may begin to occupy the building when a minimum of 3000 cu ft of outside air per square foot of floor area has been provided to the building. Once the building is occupied, it shall be ventilated with outside air at a minimum of 0.3 cfm per square foot of floor area. During each day of the flush-out period, ventilation shall begin one hour prior to occupancy and continue during occupancy. These conditions shall be maintained until 14,000 cu ft of outside air per square foot of floor area has been delivered to the space.

   What changes, if any, must be made to the plan in order to meet this option's requirements and achieve EQ Credit 3.2?

28. EQ Credit 4.3, Low-Emitting Materials: Carpet Systems is meant to reduce the quantity of volatile organic compounds (VOCs) released by carpet systems installed in building interiors. The USGBC uses the Carpet and Rug Institute's (CRI's) Green Label Plus program as a reference standard. How does the CRI measure the VOCs for this credit?

29. The project team is working with a daylighting lab and will be conducting a daylight simulation model. What daylight criteria must be used for each applicable space in order to determine the proper daylight levels when preparing to document regularly occupied spaces for EQ Credit 8.1, Daylight and Views: Daylight 75% of Spaces?

30. The lighting designer is working to provide a lighting control system to maximize energy efficiency and comply with EQ Credit 6.1, Controllability of Systems: Lighting. The current design calls for all task lighting to have user-adjustable, multi-level lighting and automatic shut-off. The budget dictates that the project team must provide design alternatives that provide the owner with up-front cost savings in order to meet budget constraints. Discuss possible modifications to the lighting controls that will still meet the requirements of EQ Credit 6.1.

31. The office building owners have directed the design team to provide thermal conditions to maximize the building occupants' comfort and productivity. As part of this effort, the mechanical engineer is designing an HVAC system that will meet the requirements of EQ Credit 6.2, Controllability of Systems: Thermal Comfort. What standard in the LEED-NC Rating System is referenced for thermal comfort? What

thermal comfort control system condition must be controlled by the building occupants?

32. The design team is working with daylighting consultants to achieve a point for EQ Credit 8.2, Daylight and Views: Views for 90% of Spaces. What types of spaces are considered to be regularly occupied according to the USGBC? Explain one design strategy the project team can implement to achieve a point for EQ Credit 8.2.

Innovation and Design Process

33. During what stage is it necessary to document ID Credit 2, LEED Accredited Professional?

34. List two potential exemplary performance strategies based on the project scenario. Explain how each meets the requirements for ID Credit 1, Innovation in Design for Exemplary Performance.

35. List two potential innovative performance strategies based on the project scenario. Explain how each meets the requirements for ID Credit 1, Innovation in Design for Innovative Strategies.

Downtown Office Building Solutions

Sustainable Sites

1. To demonstrate compliance with SS Credit 2, Development Density and Community Connectivity, the project team must prove that the project's development density is a minimum of 60,000 sq ft per acre, *and* that the project site is constructed in a community with surrounding site development density of 60,000 sq ft per acre.

    Calculate the project site development density to see if it meets the minimum requirement of 60,000 sq ft/ac.

    $$\text{development density} = \frac{\text{gross building square footage}}{\text{project site area}}$$
    $$= \frac{225{,}000 \text{ ft}^2}{0.38 \text{ ac}}$$
    $$= 592{,}105 \text{ ft}^2/\text{ac}$$

    The development density for this project exceeds the minimum requirement of 60,000 sq ft/ac.

    Understand how to determine the density radius.

    $$\text{density radius} = 3\sqrt{\text{project site area}}$$
    $$= 3\sqrt{(0.38 \text{ ac})\left(43{,}560 \, \frac{\text{ft}^2}{\text{ac}}\right)}$$
    $$= 386 \text{ ft}$$

    To calculate the surrounding site development density, first find the surrounding site area. (Note: The undeveloped site area must be converted from square feet to acres.)

$$\text{surrounding site area} = \text{total site area within density radius} - \text{undeveloped site area}$$

$$= 10.8 \text{ ac} - \frac{150{,}000 \text{ ft}^2}{43{,}560 \frac{\text{ft}^2}{\text{ac}}}$$

$$= 7.356 \text{ ac}$$

$$\text{surrounding site development density} = \frac{\text{total building area within density radius}}{\text{surrounding site area}}$$

$$= \frac{850{,}000 \text{ ft}^2}{7.356 \text{ ac}}$$

$$= 115{,}552 \text{ ft}^2/\text{ac} \quad (116{,}000 \text{ ft}^2/\text{ac})$$

The surrounding site development density for this project exceeds the minimum 60,000 sq ft/ac requirement. The project team has demonstrated compliance with both density requirements of SS Credit 2.

2. The owners or project team must seek out a local, state, or federal agency to classify the site as a brownfield. According to USGBC, a private consultant on the design team does not have the ability to classify a site as a brownfield.

3. To achieve SS Credit 4.2, Alternative Transportation: Bicycle Storage and Changing Rooms, a commercial building must provide secure bicycle racks and/or storage for 5% or more of all building users (measured at peak periods), and provide changing and showering facilities for 0.5% of full-time equivalent (FTE) occupants.

a. Use the following equation to find the number of FTE occupants.

$$\text{FTE occupants} = \frac{\text{occupant hours}}{8 \text{ hr}}$$

$$= \frac{7032 \text{ occupant-hr}}{8 \text{ hr}}$$

$$= 879 \text{ occupants}$$

b. To find the number of required secure bicycle spaces, first find the number of peak building users.

$$\text{peak building users} = \text{FTE occupants} + \text{transient occupants}$$

$$= 879 \text{ occupants} + 84 \text{ occupants}$$

$$= 963 \text{ users}$$

Then calculate the number of secure bicycle spaces.

$$\text{secure bicycle spaces} = (\text{peak building users})(0.05)$$

$$= (963 \text{ users})(0.05)$$

$$= 48.15 \text{ spaces} \quad (49 \text{ spaces})$$

c. Calculate the minimum number of changing and showering facilities.

$$\text{showering facilities} = (\text{FTE occupants})(0.005)$$
$$= (879 \text{ occupants})(0.005)$$
$$= 4.39 \text{ facilities} \quad (5 \text{ facilities})$$

4. To obtain SS Credit 4.3, Alternative Transportation: Low-Emission and Fuel Efficient Vehicles, Option 2, the project team must allocate 5% of the site's total vehicle parking capacity to low-emission and fuel-efficient vehicles. There are 300 parking spaces included in the design of this project. Therefore,

$$\text{preferred parking spaces} = (300 \text{ spaces})(0.05) = 15 \text{ spaces}$$

The new project design must allocate 15 preferred parking spaces to alternative fuel vehicles in order to receive a point for SS Credit 4.3.

5. SS Credit 4.4, Alternative Transportation: Parking Capacity, Option 2 applies to non-residential projects that provide parking for less than 5% of FTE building occupants. It would require the project to provide preferred parking for carpools or vanpools, marked as such, for 5% of total provided parking spaces. To determine if Option 2 is a viable choice for this project, calculate the quantity of spaces needed for 5% of the FTE building occupants.

$$\text{FTE occupants} = \frac{\text{occupant hours}}{8 \text{ hr}}$$
$$= \frac{7032 \text{ occupant-hr}}{8 \text{ hr}}$$
$$= 879 \text{ occupants}$$

Then determine if the total number of provided parking spaces is less than 5% of FTE occupants.

$$5\% \text{ of FTE} = (879 \text{ occupants})(0.05)$$
$$= 43.95 \quad (44)$$

Option 2 is not a viable choice for the project as long as the project design calls for 300 parking spaces, as 300 exceeds the maximum allowable number of spaces stipulated by SS Credit 4.4, Option 2 (5% of the FTE building occupants, or 44).

6. To achieve SS Credit 5.1, Site Development: Protect or Restore Habitat, the project team must restore or protect a minimum of 50% of the site area, excluding the building footprint, with native or adapted vegetation. Since this project has earned a point for SS Credit 2, Development Density and Community Connectivity, and is using a vegetated roof surface, the team may apply the vegetated roof surface to the calculation if the plants meet the definition of native or adapted. The USGBC defines native or adapted plants as plants indigenous to a locality, or as cultivars of native plants that are adapted to the local climate and are not considered invasive species or noxious weeds.

7. SS Credit 7.1, Heat Island Effect: Non-Roof, Option 2 is most appropriate for the office building because its parking structure will be located underground. Option 2 requires that a project have a minimum of 50% of its parking spaces under a roof cover with an SRI of at least 29. The USGBC defines under cover as underground, under deck, under roof, or under a building. Since 100% of the parking for this project will be located underground, it achieves SS Credit 7.1. Additionally, the office building is also eligible for an exemplary performance point for this credit.

8. In order to achieve SS Credit 7.2, Heat Island Effect: Roof, the project team should choose Option 2 because the project scenario states a vegetated roof will cover the majority of the roof surface. Option 2 requires the installation of a vegetated roof for at least 50% of the roof area. The total roof area excludes mechanical equipment, photovoltaic panels, and skylights.

Water Efficiency

9. According to the *LEED-NC Reference Guide*, the landscape coefficient (K_L) indicates the volume of water lost via evapotranspiration. It is dependent on the landscape species or species factor (k_s), the microclimate or microclimate factor (k_{mc}), and the planting density or density factor (k_d). The landscape coefficient can be calculated from the following equation.

$$K_L = k_s k_d k_{mc}$$

10. The Energy Policy Act (EPACT) of 1992 is the standard referenced by WE Credit 3, Water Use Reduction. The EPACT addresses energy and water use in commercial, institutional, and residential buildings. The water fixture performance requirements include lavatory faucets, kitchen sinks, showers, hand wash fountains, janitor sinks, water closets, and urinals. The EPACT fixture flow requirements are: water closets at 1.6 gal/flush (gpf), urinals at 1.0 gpf, shower heads at 2.5 gal per minute (gpm), lavatory faucets at 2.5 gpm, replacement aerators at 2.5 gpm, and metering faucets at 0.25 gal per cycle.

Energy and Atmosphere

11. The following building components must meet ASHRAE/IESNA Standard 90.1-2004 in order for the project to obtain EA Prerequisite 2, Minimum Energy Performance.

- building envelope
- heating, ventilating, and air-conditioning systems
- service water heating
- power
- lighting
- other equipment (including all permanently wired electrical motors)

12. The new office building is reusing the building's original HVAC&R equipment. In order to comply with EA Prerequisite 3, Fundamental Refrigerant Management, the project team must confirm it has a phase-out plan for any CFC-based equipment in the base building HVAC&R and fire suppression systems. This confirmation must include a narrative description of the phase-out plan with dates and refrigerant quantities as a percentage of the overall project equipment. Since the building is connected to a chilled water system, the system must be CFC-free, or there must be a commitment to be CFC-free within five years of the substantial completion of the construction project. During the five year period, CFC-based refrigerant leakage must be 5% or less.

13. EA Credit 1, Optimize Energy Performance, Option 1 is a whole building energy simulation worth 1–10 points based on performance relative to ASHRAE 90.1-2004 (without amendments) and is applicable to this project because it does not limit a building's type or size. This option is based on energy costs associated with the project, and it compares the energy cost calculated for the proposed building design to a baseline building design modeled after minimum ASHRAE 90.1-2004 standards. The whole building energy simulation model uses the building performance rating method in Appendix G of this standard.

    A whole building energy simulation will help maximize the applied daylighting strategies, as well as examine options for the chilled water system. The simulation will also examine other building systems for viable alternatives in maximizing the efficiency of the building.

14. Demand reduction is an energy performance strategy that optimizes the schedule of regulated building systems by shifting energy loads to off-peak periods. One result of shifting energy loads to off-peak periods is lower utility bills because utility companies typically charge higher rates during peak periods. This demand reduction is reflected in the building performance method in EA Credit 1, Optimize Energy Performance. In this credit, the percentage of energy efficiency is a function of the total annual energy cost.

    This project has the capability to incorporate demand reduction in several ways. One technique mentioned in the project scenario is daylight harvesting. Daylighting techniques help reduce energy consumption by turning off lights during peak periods, and during the mid-afternoon when natural light is readily available and employees are still working in their offices. Using modeling programs and collaboration with daylighting labs will accomplish this goal.

    Because this is an existing building, its overall orientation cannot be adjusted. However, the building form and envelope can be designed and constructed to reduce heating and cooling demands during peak periods. Additionally, the project can reduce demand by using nighttime cooling, a technique where energy use is shifted to off-peak periods and stored for use during peak periods.

15. EA Credit 1, Optimize Energy Performance, Option 1—Whole Building Energy Simulation, uses the performance rating method to calculate the total energy that is consumed in a building. This determines the building's annual energy cost. The performance rating method breaks out values for energy consumption by fuel type

based on a dollar value. In order to calculate the renewable energy cost (REC), the project team must assign a dollar value to the energy created by the proposed photovoltaics. The energy rate is determined using a local utility rate, or by dividing the annual energy cost data by the annual energy consumption data from the whole building energy simulation. Multiplying the energy rate by the predicted energy output of the photovoltaic system will determine the REC.

Percentage of on-site renewable energy can be calculated from the following equation.

$$\% \text{ on-site renewable energy} = \frac{\text{REC}}{\text{building annual energy cost}} \times 100\%$$

16. The project team may need to consider a trade-off when it analyzes the application of credits EA Credit 1, Optimize Energy Performance and EA Credit 4, Enhanced Refrigerant Management. EA Credit 1, Option 1 gives points for the energy efficiency of the building and its equipment. The associated energy consumption of the building has an indirect impact on global warming. EA Credit 4 gives a point for reducing ozone depleting compounds and greenhouse gases in HVAC&R equipment. The refrigeration equipment referenced in EA Credit 4 has a direct impact on ozone depletion and global warming.

The thermodynamic properties vary among different refrigerants and therefore, require more or less electricity to produce the building's cooling. The same amount of cooling may require more electricity. This has an impact on the energy efficiency of the building and power plant emissions of greenhouse gases. There will also be cost implications for high performance HVAC&R equipment. In this case, the design team may need to make a decision based on the owner's input to comply with EA Credit 4 or to maximize EA Credit 1.

17. The USGBC LEED-NC Rating System specifies there are three acceptable approaches to achieving EA Credit 6, Green Power. The first approach is appropriate for states with open electrical markets. In this approach, the owner must secure a two-year contract for a minimum of 35% of their simulated or estimated annual power consumption from a Green-e certified provider according to the Department of Energy (DOE) Commercial Building Energy Consumption Survey (CBECS). (Note: the Green-e program is administered by the Center for Resource Solutions (CRS), which operates national and international programs that support the use of renewable energy sources. To find a Green-e certified provider or to learn more about the Green-e program, go to the Green-e website at www.green-e.org.)

The second approach is appropriate for states with a closed electrical market. The governing utility may have a Green-e accredited utility program. Again, the owner must secure a two-year contract for a minimum of 35% of their annual power consumption from a Green-e certified provider.

The third approach is appropriate when direct purchase of Green-e certified power is not available through the local utilities. The team may also purchase Green-e accredited Renewable Energy Certificates (REC) also referred to as Green Tags, Tradable Renewable Certificates (TRC), Green Credits, or Renewable Energy Credits. The team must purchase RECs equivalent to 35% of the predicted annual power consumption over a two-year period.

Materials and Resources

18. LEED-NC applies to new construction and major renovations, while LEED-EB is designed for building operations, processes, system upgrades, and minor space-use changes. LEED-EB can also be used for buildings that have been previously certified with the LEED-NC Rating System.

The LEED-NC Rating System is most appropriate because this project will be retrofitting an existing 13,235 sq ft warehouse, while the addition will be over 200,000 sq ft.

19. The downtown office building will be retrofitting an existing 13,235 sq ft warehouse and adding over 200,000 sq ft. MR Credit 1, Building Reuse states that an addition to an existing building cannot be more than two times the square footage of the existing building. Since 200,000 sq ft is greater than two times the existing building's square footage, this project does not qualify for MR Credit 1.

20. Because the downtown office building includes an addition that is greater than two times the existing building's square footage, the project cannot qualify for MR Credit 1, Building Reuse. However, the project can qualify for MR Credit 2, Construction Waste Management, which requires a project to divert materials from the landfill. The reused existing building's materials may be included in the calculations for MR Credit 2.

21. To achieve MR Credit 3, Materials Reuse, the general contractor must, at a minimum, document and submit the following information.

- description of the material (i.e., salvaged wood floor)

- source or vendor of the material (i.e., on-site salvaged and refurbished)

- value (based on replacement value) or material cost

22. Removing and recycling the asphalt from an existing parking lot does not meet the intent or the requirements of MR Credit 4, Recycled Content. While the general contractor's strategy does reduce impacts from extraction and processing virgin materials, it does not increase the demand for building products that incorporate recycled content materials. MR Credit 4 provides points for projects that use materials with post-consumer and pre-consumer recycled content.

However, removing, recycling, and reusing the asphalt on a different project does contribute to other LEED credits. This project can earn points under MR Credit 2, Construction Waste Management, for materials that are diverted from the landfill.

23. Reusing the existing building's doors as light shelves will, or will not, apply to the following credits.

a. *MR Credit 1, Building Reuse*: The reuse of doors as light shelves will not apply to MR Credit 1. This project does not qualify for MR Credit 1 because the square footage of the addition is more than two times the existing building's square footage.

b. *MR Credit 2, Construction Waste Management*: The reuse of doors as light shelves will apply to MR Credit 2 because this project did not qualify for MR Credit 1. The reused door materials will be diverted from the landfill. However, the reused doors cannot simultaneously qualify for MR Credit 2 and MR Credit 3, Materials Reuse. A decision must be made as to which credit the reused doors will apply.

c. *MR Credit 3, Materials Reuse*: The reuse of doors as light shelves will contribute towards MR Credit 3. Because the project did not qualify for MR Credit 1, any reused materials from the existing building can be used in the calculation of this credit. Qualifying materials include those found on site, in the existing building, or at a different location. As previously stated, materials applied to MR Credit 2 cannot also be applied to MR Credit 3, so the project team must decide which credit the reused doors will be applied to.

d. *MR Credit 5, Regional Materials*: The reuse of doors as light shelves will apply to MR Credit 5. The doors were extracted from the existing building and were resurfaced and treated within 500 mi of the site.

e. *EA Credit 1, Optimize Energy Performance*: The reuse of doors as light shelves will apply to EA Credit 1 by reducing energy consumption. The light shelves will provide a better distribution of daylight and reduce the need for electric lighting during the day. They will also reduce unwanted direct solar heat gain, reducing the need for cooling during the summer. However, a more effective approach to controlling unwanted solar heat gain is using shading devices that reduce the solar heat gain from entering the building. Shading devices are mounted to the exterior of the building and light shelves are installed on the interior of the building.

f. *EQ Credit 8.1, Daylight and Views: Daylight 75% of Spaces*: If the project team uses Option 1—Glazing Factor Calculation, the reuse of doors as light shelves will contribute to the achievement of EQ Credit 8.1, but will not contribute to the option's glazing factor calculation. Option 1 requires that each window has a glare control device, such as a light shelf. If the project team uses Option 2—Daylight Simulation Model, or Option 3—Daylight Measurement, the light shelves will aid in the achievement of EQ Credit 8.1. The light shelves will help distribute the daylight further into the building and provide a more uniform illumination level.

g. *EQ Credit 8.2, Daylight and Views: Views for 90% of Spaces*: The reuse of doors as light shelves will not contribute to EQ Credit 8.2. The intent of this credit is to provide the occupants of a building with a connection to the outdoors through outside views. While the light shelves will help distribute and control daylight and help reduce unwanted direct solar heat gain, the light shelves will not create a view to the outdoors.

Indoor Environmental Quality

24. To meet the requirements of EQ Prerequisite 1, Minimum IAQ Performance, the project team must first determine if the space is mechanically ventilated, naturally ventilated, or mixed-mode ventilated. The project's general information states that the office building will be mechanically ventilated. Therefore, it must comply with the minimum requirements of ASHRAE 62.1-2004, Ventilation for Acceptable Indoor Air Quality, Secs. 4–7. The project team must demonstrate that the mechanical systems provide the minimum outdoor airflow for each zone and the outdoor air intake flow for the system meets, or exceeds, the requirements of ASHRAE 62.1-2004.

25. The design criterion for densely occupied spaces does not meet the parameters of EQ Credit 1, Outdoor Air Delivery Monitoring. For mechanically ventilated spaces, densely occupied spaces are defined as 25 people per 1000 sq ft. Therefore, the design criterion for the HVAC systems must decrease from 30 people per 1000 sq ft, to 25 people per 1000 sq ft. However, the CO_2 sensors are located properly in the vertical breathing zone according to LEED and ASHRAE standards.

    The non-densely occupied criterion also fails to meet EQ Credit 1 requirements. As defined by ASHRAE-62.1-2004, outdoor airflow monitors must be capable of measuring the minimum outdoor air flow rate with an accuracy of plus or minus 15%, not 20%, of the design minimum outdoor air rate.

26. When permanent air handlers are used during construction, the filtration media must have a minimum efficiency reporting value (MERV) of eight at each return grill, as determined by ASHRAE 52.2-1999. MERV provides a standard in filtration media that is based on three composite average particle size removal efficiency points. MERV ratings indicate how efficient a filter is at removing particulates from the air. The higher a MERV rating is, the better the filter is at removing these particulates. However, higher MERV ratings decrease a building's mechanical ventilation systems energy efficiency due to filtration density. The LEED-NC Rating System requires that all filtration media used during construction must be replaced prior to occupancy in order to reduce indoor air quality (IAQ) problems resulting from the construction process.

27. The LEED AP has made the following changes to the plan submitted by the project team based on the requirements in the LEED-NC Rating System for EQ Credit 3.2, Construction IAQ Management Plan: Before Occupancy. Changes are italicized.

    The owners have stated their desire to occupy the building at the earliest possible date. The owners may begin to occupy the building when a minimum of *3500* cu ft of outside air per square foot of floor area has been provided to the building. Once the building is occupied, it shall be ventilated with outside air at a minimum of 0.3 cfm per square foot of floor area, *or the design minimum outside air rate as determined in EQ Perquisite 1, whichever is greater.* During each day of the flush-out period, ventilation shall begin *three hours* prior to occupancy and continue during occupancy. These conditions shall be maintained until 14,000 cu ft of outside air per square foot of floor area has been delivered to the space.

28. The Carpet and Rug Institute (CRI) measures volatile organic compound (VOC) *emissions* in micrograms per square meter per hour. Other reference standards, such as the South Coast Air Quality Management District (SCAQMD), measure VOC *content* in grams per liter. Note that EQ Credit 4.1, Low-Emitting Materials: Adhesives and Sealants, and EQ Credit 4.2, Low-Emitting Materials: Paints and Coatings, reference standards that measure VOC *content*, not VOC *emissions*.

29. In order to document EQ Credit 8.1, Daylight and Views: Daylight 75% of Spaces, the project team's daylight simulation model must use the following *LEED-NC Reference Guide* criteria.

    - Clear sky conditions at noon on the equinox (around March 21 and September 21).

    - Calculations must be taken at 30 in above the floor, which corresponds to a typical work plane height.

30. Possible modifications to the office building's lighting control system include the elimination of all multi-level lighting and automatic shut-off features. However, according to the minimum requirements of EQ Credit 6.1, Controllability of Systems: Lighting, the system must maintain on and off control for all task lighting. Optimal lighting control systems provide the user with multiple levels of control, which adds to occupant comfort and maximizes efficiency. However, this level of control does increase cost due to added equipment. (Note: It is important to consider local energy code compliance when determining task lighting control strategies.)

31. The LEED-NC Rating System identifies ASHRAE 55-2004 as a reference standard for thermal comfort. This standard states air temperature, radiant temperature, air speed, and humidity are the primary factors that affect thermal comfort. In order to comply with EQ Credit 6.2, Controllability of Systems: Thermal Comfort, the thermal control system must allow the occupant to control one or more of these conditions in the occupant's local environment.

32. The USGBC considers regularly occupied spaces to include office spaces, conference rooms, and cafeterias. Spaces considered to be non-regularly occupied are support areas such as mechanical equipment rooms, laundry, corridors, hallways, lobbies, break rooms, copy rooms, kitchens, stairwells, and restrooms. Spaces considered non-occupied include storage and equipment rooms, closets, and janitorial rooms.

The majority of the building's regularly occupied spaces are a combination of private and open offices. EQ Credit 8.2, Daylight and Views: Views for 90% of Spaces requires 90% of regularly occupied spaces to have a direct line of sight to the outdoors using vision glazing. Vision glazing must be 2 ft 6 in to 7 ft 6 in above the finished floor. To achieve this credit, the project team can design the building so that open offices are located along the building's perimeter walls to maximize occupant views to the outdoor environment. Private offices can be located in the central core of the building and use interior glass so that occupants can share the view to the outdoors with the open offices. The design team may also choose to locate support areas and non-regularly occupied spaces in the central core areas of the building.

Innovation and Design Process

33. It is necessary to document ID Credit 2, LEED Accredited Professional in the construction submittal stage. The LEED AP must be a primary member of the design team.

Note: The following Innovation and Design Process solutions are based on hypothetical project scenarios and were derived from researching past Innovation in Design Credit Interpretation Rulings. These suggested innovations have not been formally submitted to the USGBC for approval. Therefore, if pursuing any of the following innovations, it is recommended one research current Innovation in Design Credit Interpretation Rulings, or submit Credit Interpretation Requests to the USGBC.

34. ID Credit 1, Innovation in Design for Exemplary Performance, provides design teams the opportunity to be awarded points for exceptional performance above the requirements set by the LEED-NC Rating System. Exemplary performance ID credits are generally awarded for doubling the credit requirements and/or achieving the next incremental percentage threshold. Based on the project scenario, the following options provide two potential opportunities to achieve ID Credit 1.

Option 1—MR Credit 2, Construction Waste Management—Exemplary Performance: The office building will not qualify for MR Credit 1, Building Reuse, but the materials that are reused can be applied to MR Credit 2, Construction Waste Management. If the project can attain a 95% diversion rate from the landfill, it will exceed the 75% diversion rate required by MR Credit 2. Attaining a 95% diversion rate meets the exemplary performance threshold stated in the *LEED-NC Reference Guide*.

Option 2—SS Credit 7.1, Heat Island Effect: Non-Roof—Exemplary Performance: The project scenario states that all parking is located underground which is considered exemplary performance. The office building substantially exceeds the base criteria of 50%, as stated in the SS Credit 7.1 requirements.

35. ID Credit 1, Innovation in Design for Innovative Performance, provides design teams the opportunity to be awarded points for innovative performance outside of the requirements set by the LEED-NC Rating System. Innovative performance ID credits are generally awarded for comprehensive strategies that demonstrate significant and quantifiable environmental and/or health benefits. Based on the project scenario, the following options are two potential opportunities to achieve ID Credit 1.

Option 1—Toxic Material Source Reduction—Innovative Performance: The project will use low-mercury lamps throughout the facility and will meet the criteria set forth in LEED-Existing Buildings (LEED EB), MR Prerequisite 2. It is a viable option to pursue credits or prerequisites that are recognized by other LEED rating systems for innovation credits in the LEED-NC Rating System. The design team will submit a policy that states all future purchases of mercury-containing lamps will be made in such a way that the average mercury content is less than the specified levels of 90 picograms/lumen-hr. Calculations must show the total mercury content, the total lumen hours of light output, the total number and type of lamps, and the overall weighted average mercury content for all lamps in units of picograms/lumen-hr. In these calculations, rated hours of lamp life are defined by the manufacturer and are based on the design, or mean light output, of the lamps. The mean light output in lumens is the light output at 40% of lamp life.

Option 2—Indoor Air Quality: Green Housekeeping—Innovative Performance: In order to receive a point for innovative performance, the program's housekeeping policies and environmental cleaning solution specifications must be documented. The project team must demonstrate that a comprehensive green cleaning and housekeeping program is in place. The program should have have clear performance goals, including the following.

   a. A statement of purpose describing what the policy is trying to achieve from a health and environmental standpoint. At a minimum, the policy should focus on types of cleaning chemicals and provide a description of custodial training.

   b. A contractual or procedural requirement for operations staff to comply with the guidelines, including a written program for training and implementation.

   c. A clear set of acceptable performance level standards by which to measure progress or achievement, such as Green Seal standard GS-37 (go to www.greenseal.org) or California Code of Regulations, Title 17 Section 94509, VOC standards, for cleaning products. (Go to www.calregs.com, click on California Code of Regulations, and perform a keyword search for 94509.)

d. A documentation of the program's housekeeping policies and environmental cleaning solution specifications, including a list of approved and prohibited chemicals and practices. Demonstrate that the products used are non-hazardous, have a low environmental impact, and meet the Green Seal or California Code of Regulations criteria previously described in the previous bullet. Concentrated cleaning products should be utilized when available to save resources as they use less packaging and use less energy in shipping the product.

Furniture Manufacturing Facility Problems

3

Vicinity Plan

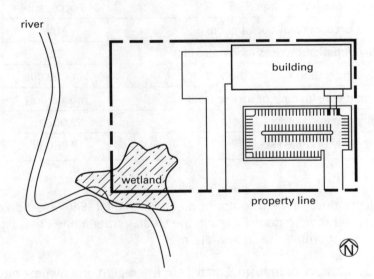

river

building

wetland

property line

Scenario

An existing 36,000 sq ft cold storage warehouse in Titletown, Wisconsin is being renovated into a furniture manufacturing facility. The new building will reuse the existing building and will include a 40,000 sq ft addition in order to create office spaces and a product showroom. The project site contains wetlands that are 200 ft away from all structures in the new development, and the southwest boundary of the project site is located 75 ft away from an adjacent property's stream. The owners have elected to purchase half of the factory's total power from a Green-e certified source and have instructed the project design team to include as many materials with local and recycled content as the budget will allow.

The warehouse will be retrofitted with skylights to provide daylight. Heat recovered from the manufacturing process will be used to heat the building during the cooler months, and the heat recovery process will contribute to preheating the process water. Due to budget and time constraints, the project team will not perform energy modeling to document differences between the project's baseline design and proposed design.

In an effort to be a model business in a community where water quality issues are prevalent from a history of industrial waste, the manufacturing plant has committed to treating 100% of wastewater on site. The owners have partnered with a local nonprofit agency that has received government funding to limit industrial pollution. This third-party funding will support the on-site treatment of wastewater and the implementation of a vegetated roof. The vegetated roof is a stormwater management strategy that treats and reduces the stormwater runoff. Additionally, the site's parking lot will utilize grid pavement with bioswales to also treat runoff.

General Information	
project building footprint	65,000 ft^2
gross building square footage	76,000 ft^2
project site area	3.8 ac
occupant hours (at peak period)	216 occupant-hr
transient occupants (at peak period)	6
quantity of parking spaces (non-preferred)	32
overall construction cost (divisions 2–10)	$11,400,000
ventilation type (natural or mechanical)	mechanical
regularly occupied spaces	57,000 ft^2
non-regularly occupied spaces	19,000 ft^2

Sustainable Sites

1. Does the project's development footprint meet SS Credit 1, Site Selection's wetland and bodies of water requirements? Explain the credit's criteria and describe what the project team must submit if the criteria are met.

2. Since there was a history of industrial activity in the region, the owners believe their property could be classified as a brownfield. What type of assessment is needed to document a contaminated site in order to achieve SS Credit 3, Brownfield Redevelopment?

3. How many secure bicycle spaces and changing and showering facilities are required to meet SS Credit 4.2, Alternative Transportation: Bicycle Storage and Changing Rooms? Complete the following calculations.

    a. Find the number of full-time equivalent (FTE) occupants.

    b. Find the number of required secure bicycle spaces.

    c. Find the number of required changing and showering facilities.

4. The project design team is pursuing SS Credit 4.3, Alternative Transportation: Low-Emission and Fuel Efficient Vehicles, Option 1. How many low-emission, fuel efficient vehicles *and* preferred parking spaces must be provided in order to achieve SS Credit 4.3?

5. Use the following information to describe how this project can earn one point for SS Credit 5.2, Site Development: Maximize Open Space.

    a. There are no requirements for open space in Titletown's local industrial zoning ordinances.

    b. The project design earned SS Credit 2: Development Density and Community Connectivity via Option 2—Community Connectivity.

    c. The undeveloped site area is 30,548 sq ft, of which 8120 sq ft is a vegetated wet land area with a gradient average of 1:4.

    d. The building footprint is 65,000 sq ft with a vegetated roof covering 54,300 sq ft.

    e. The grid pavement parking area is 50,560 sq ft.

    f. The asphalt and concrete covered area is 19,420 sq ft.

6. The project design team is deciding which strategies will be the most effective in achieving points for SS Credit 6.1, Stormwater Design: Quantity Control. What is the most effective strategy the project team can utilize to minimize the volume of stormwater runoff and achieve this credit?

7. The project design team is completing calculations for SS Credit 6.2, Stormwater Design: Quality Control. Since there are wetlands on the project site and a stream adjacent to the site, the team is committed to the requirements of this credit. What stormwater control criteria must be met for the stormwater control measures that discharge water off site?

8. The project team will be retrofitting the warehouse with skylights to provide daylight inside the building. The project team is creating plans to install electric lighting in the skylights to create a nighttime glowing effect. The owners have directed the project team to comply with SS Credit 8, Light Pollution Reduction. Will this lighting strategy prevent achieving this credit? Explain why or why not.

Water Efficiency

9. The assistance of third-party funding enables the manufacturing plant to treat 100% of wastewater on site. However, if this funding falls through, the owners would still like to meet WE Credit 2, Innovative Wastewater Technologies. What alternative green building strategies could the project design team employ to achieve this credit? What data must the team track and compile in order to complete wastewater calculations for this credit?

10. There are many green building strategies that interact and combine to create credit synergies. State three credits that are directly impacted by the landscape design. How could these credits be seen as a synergy with WE Credit 1, Water Efficient Landscaping?

Energy and Atmosphere

11. Due to budget and time constraints, the project team will not perform energy modeling. What forms must the project team submit to meet EA Prerequisite 2, Minimum Energy Performance?

12. The project design team is working to achieve EA Credit 1, Optimize Energy Performance via Option 2. Describe this option and determine if the project team will meet its criteria.

13. The project scenario discusses how the manufacturing facility will incorporate waste energy recovery. To which EA credit does waste energy recovery apply? Can the project design earn points under this EA credit?

14. A project team can choose from four options to qualify for EA Credit 1, Optimize Energy Performance. As a potential cost savings measure, the project design team is considering pursuing Option 3. Describe this option and determine if it is applicable to this project.

15. The project design team is trying to design a biomass renewable energy system based on the waste-stream materials within the building. What materials are considered eligible as a bio-fuel based on requirements of EA Credit 2, On-Site Renewable Energy?

16. EA Credit 3, Enhanced Commissioning requires a basis of design (BOD). Describe a BOD and how it relates to the enhanced commissioning process.

17. The project team is trying to maximize the number of LEED points its design can achieve and would like to comply with EA Credit 4, Enhanced Refrigerant Management. How will this credit affect the design of the building's HVAC&R systems? Explain how using natural ventilation in the manufacturing facility and eliminating air conditioning will affect this credit.

18. The design team is estimating the electrical consumption of the building in order to determine the amount of Green-e certified power to purchase and document for compliance with EA Credit 6, Green Power. What is the required annual minimum green power purchase for this project?

Materials and Resources

19. According to the requirements of MR Credit 1, Building Reuse, explain why this project does or does not qualify for this credit.

20. What existing building elements are excluded from the calculations for MR Credit 1.1 and MR Credit 1.2, Building Reuse?

21. The project will qualify for MR Credit 1.1, Building Reuse: Maintain 75% of Existing Walls, Floors, and Roof, but will not qualify for MR Credit 1.2, Building Reuse: Maintain 95% of Existing Walls, Floors, and Roof. Can this project still qualify for MR Credit 1.3, Maintain 50% of Interior Non-Structural Elements? Explain why or why not.

22. Explain how to calculate the following building elements in order to meet the requirements of MR Credit 1.3, Building Reuse: Maintain 50% of Interior Non-Structural Elements.

    a. finished ceilings/flooring

    b. interior non-structural walls

    c. interior doors

    d. interior casework

23. The project design has achieved MR Credit 1.1, Building Reuse: Maintain 75% of Existing Walls, Floors, and Roof. Can the design also achieve MR Credit 2, Construction Waste Management and MR Credit 3, Materials Reuse?

24. During the excavation process, the project site's soil was found to be contaminated by two buried petroleum tanks. The project team earned a point for SS Credit 3, Brownfield Redevelopment by documenting that the petroleum tanks were recycled, and the contaminated soil was cleaned and used for site preparation materials at another job site. Does the removal of the contaminated soil contribute to MR Credit 2, Construction Waste Management? Explain why or why not.

25. The project's general contractor has been documenting the construction waste diversion rate and feels it will be possible to not only meet requirements for both MR Credit 2.1 and MR Credit 2.2, but to surpass the requirements of both credits by a considerable amount. What percentage of total construction waste must be diverted from the landfill or incineration in order to earn an Innovation in Design point for MR Credit 2, Construction Waste Management?

26. The project design team would like to earn a point for MR Credit 6, Rapidly Renewable Materials. Explain how the value of rapidly renewable materials is calculated. Using the 45% default materials value, what is the minimum dollar amount of rapidly renewable materials necessary to earn a point for MR Credit 6?

Indoor Environmental Quality

27. Due to Titletown's extreme winter temperatures, the building owners would like to include a designated indoor smoking area for their employees. What are the design criteria for non-residential buildings that include indoor smoking areas, as required by EQ Prerequisite 2, Environmental Tobacco Smoke (ETS) Control?

28. The owners want to maximize the quantity of fresh outdoor air in the building to improve the comfort, well-being, and productivity of their employees and so are applying EQ Credit 2, Increased Ventilation to the project design. How will the application of this credit impact the energy efficiency of the building?

29. The flooring contractor for the project has submitted a Material Safety and Data Sheet (MSDS) for the adhesive used for the rubber flooring. The MSDS indicates that the volatile organic compound (VOC) content for the adhesive is 65 g/L. The project design team would like to meet the requirements for EQ Credit 4.1, Low-Emitting

Materials: Adhesives and Sealants. What standard does this credit reference and does this adhesive meet its criteria?

30. The interior designer and general contractor submitted a request for information in order to determine the project's volatile organic compound (VOC) paint limits. For the following paint applications, provide VOC limits as stated in the LEED-NC Rating System for EQ Credit 4.2, Low-Emitting Materials: Paints and Coatings.

    a. architectural paints, flats

    b. architectural paints, non-flats

    c. anti-rust paints

    d. wood stains

    e. exterior wood stains

31. The project team is committed to indoor environmental quality and wants to reduce the amount of indoor contaminants resulting from the carpet system's installation. EQ Credit 4.3, Low-Emitting Materials: Carpets Systems is meant to reduce the quantity of volatile organic compounds (VOCs) that are released by carpet systems within the interior of the environment. What three systems must be documented to comply with this credit's criteria in order to receive a point from the LEED-NC Rating System? Which referenced standards are used by these three systems?

32. The project team is working toward earning points for EQ Credit 7.1, Thermal Comfort: Design. What task(s) must be completed during the planning and design phase?

33. The building owners wish to minimize employee complaints about thermal comfort. Knowing that every individual has unique thermal requirements, the owners have required the mechanical HVAC system to provide each private office with an individual control that enables the employee to vary the temperature by a five degree temperature swing. What strategies can be used to meet the owners' requirements and the criteria of EQ Credit 6.2, Controllability of Systems: Thermal Comfort?

34. One year after the project's completion, the mechanical engineer and facilities manager for the project are completing a Plan for Corrective Action in accordance with EQ Credit 7.2 Thermal Comfort: Verification. What type of corrective actions can be included?

Innovation and Design Process

35. List two potential exemplary performance strategies based on the project scenario. Explain how each meets requirements for ID Credit 1, Innovation in Design for Exemplary Performance.

36. List two potential innovative performance strategies based on the project scenario. Explain how each meets requirements for ID Credit 1, Innovation in Design for Innovative Strategies.

Furniture Manufacturing Facility Solutions

Sustainable Sites

1. SS Credit 1, Site Selection prohibits projects from developing buildings, hardscapes, roads, or parking areas on portions of a site that are within 100 ft of any wetlands (as defined by United States Code of Federal Regulations 40 CFR, Parts 230–233 and Part 22), and within 100 ft of isolated wetlands or areas of special concern identified by state or local rule; *or* that are within wetland setback distances as prescribed or defined in state or local regulations, rules, or laws (if more stringent than the SS Credit 1 100 ft setback). The project scenario states that the site's wetlands are 200 ft away from any development on the property, which meets SS Credit 1's wetland criteria.

   SS Credit 1 also prohibits projects from building on undeveloped land that is within 50 ft of a body of water (e.g., seas, lakes, rivers, streams, and tributaries). As stated in the project scenario, the project is located on a previously developed site, and the stream is located 75 ft away on an adjacent property. Therefore, the development footprint also meets SS Credit 1's criteria for bodies of water.

   The project team will need to complete the LEED-Online submittal template to confirm that the development footprint meets the requirements of SS Credit 1. To successfully complete this process, the project team must confirm that they did not develop on any of the six prohibited areas described in the credit.

2. In order to document a contaminated site for SS Credit 3, Brownfield Redevelopment, a project team must use ASTM E1903-97 Phase II Environmental Site Assessment.

3. To meet SS Credit 4.2, Alternative Transportation: Bicycle Storage and Changing Rooms, determine how many secure bicycle spaces and changing and showering facilities are required.

a. Use the following equation to find the number of FTE occupants.

$$\text{FTE occupants} = \frac{\text{occupant hours}}{8 \text{ hr}}$$

$$= \frac{216 \text{ occupant-hr}}{8 \text{ hr}}$$

$$= 27 \text{ occupants}$$

b. To find the number of required secure bicycle spaces, first find the number of peak building occupants.

$$\text{peak building occupants} = \text{FTE occupants} + \text{transient occupants}$$

$$= 27 \text{ occupants} + 6 \text{ occupants}$$

$$= 33 \text{ occupants}$$

Then calculate the number of secure bicycle spaces.

$$\text{secure bicycle spaces} = (\text{peak building occupants})(0.05)$$

$$= (33 \text{ occupants})\left(0.05 \ \frac{\text{spaces}}{\text{occupants}}\right)$$

$$= 1.65 \text{ spaces} \quad (2 \text{ spaces})$$

c. Use the following equation to find the number of required changing and showering facilities.

$$\text{showering facilities} = (\text{FTE occupants})(0.005)$$

$$= (27 \text{ occupants})\left(0.005 \ \frac{\text{facilities}}{\text{occupants}}\right)$$

$$= 0.135 \text{ facilities} \quad (1 \text{ facility})$$

Therefore, the project design must include two secure bicycle spaces and one changing and showering facility.

4. SS Credit 4.3, Alternative Transportation: Low-Emission and Fuel Efficient Vehicles, Option 1 requires a project to provide low-emission and fuel-efficient vehicles for 3% of full-time equivalent (FTE) occupants, and to provide preferred parking for these vehicles.

$$\text{FTE occupants} = \frac{\text{occupant hours}}{8 \text{ hr}}$$

$$= \frac{216 \text{ occupant-hr}}{8 \text{ hr}}$$

$$= 27 \text{ occupants}$$

The number of alternative fuel vehicles and the number of preferred parking spaces the manufacturer must supply is the FTE multiplied by 3%, which equals

$$\text{number of cars and spaces} = (27)(0.03)$$

$$= 0.81 \text{ cars and spaces} \quad (1 \text{ car and } 1 \text{ space})$$

Therefore, one low-emission, fuel efficient vehicle and one preferred parking space must be provided for this project to achieve SS Credit 4.3.

5. To earn one point for SS Credit 5.2, Site Development: Maximize Open Space, the project team must pursue Option 3 because there are no requirements for open space in Titletown's industrial zones. Option 3 requires vegetated open space equal to 20% of the project's site area.

   To determine the total open space required, use the following equation. (Note: The total project site area must be converted from acres to square feet.)

$$\text{total open space required} = (\text{total project site area})(0.20)$$
$$= (3.8 \text{ ac})(0.20)\left(43{,}560 \, \frac{\text{ft}^2}{\text{ac}}\right)$$
$$= 33{,}106 \text{ ft}^2$$

   Because this project earned SS Credit 2, the vegetated roof area can be included in the total open space calculation. Vegetated wetlands, or naturally designed ponds with side-slope gradients averaging 1:4 or less, may also count as open space. The total open space is

   total open space $= 30{,}548 \text{ ft}^2$ undeveloped site area $+ 54{,}300 \text{ ft}^2$ vegetated roof

   $$= 84{,}848 \text{ ft}^2$$

   $84{,}848 \text{ ft}^2$ total open space is greater than $33{,}106 \text{ ft}^2$ total open space required; therefore, one point is earned.

6. The most effective way for the project team to achieve SS Credit 6.1, Stormwater Design: Quantity Control is to minimize stormwater runoff by decreasing the area of impervious surfaces on site. Minimizing impervious surfaces can be accomplished by reducing the building footprint and hardscaped areas, and by installing vegetated roofs, grid pavements, or pervious pavement systems. Incorporating bioswales, rain gardens, retention ponds, and stormwater catchment systems are additional stormwater management techniques.

7. Stormwater control measures that discharge water off-site must remove 80% of the average annual post-development total suspended solids (TSS). Stormwater control measures are considered to meet this criterion if 1) they are designed in accordance with standards and specifications from a state or local program that has adopted these performance standards, or 2) there exists in-field performance monitoring data demonstrating compliance with the criteria. Data must conform to accepted protocol for best management practice monitoring.

8. If properly controlled, installing electric lighting in the skylights to create a nighttime glowing effect will not prevent the project from achieving SS Credit 8, Light Pollution Reduction. The design team must ensure the maximum candela from each luminaire located on the interior of the building intersects opaque building surfaces and does not exit through windows. If the maximum candela from each luminaire located on the interior of the building exits through a window or skylight, then an automatic lighting control system must turn these electric lights off during non-business hours in order to earn a point for SS Credit 8.

Water Efficiency

9. If the funding for wastewater treatment falls through, the design team must focus on WE Credit 2, Innovative Wastewater Technologies, Option 1. Option 1 requires a building to reduce potable water use for building sewage conveyance by 50%. Strategies include low-flow water closets, composting toilets, waterless urinals, rain water harvesting systems, graywater systems, and other strategies that reduce the need for potable water used in wastewater systems.

Blackwater-generating fixture and frequency-of-use data must be compiled to complete wastewater calculations for WE Credit 2, Option 1.

10. Innovative project teams can utilize landscape design to achieve more than one LEED credit for a particular building strategy. A synergy is a green building strategy that contributes to the achievement of more than one LEED credit. The following are possible credit synergies with WE Credit 1, Water Efficient Landscaping.

1. *SS Credit 5, Site Development*: Using native and adapted vegetation is a green building strategy that contributes to both the requirements of WE Credit 1 and SS Credit 5. The use of native and adapted vegetation helps to protect and restore damaged areas of the project site and can be planted in a site's open space.

2. *SS Credit 6, Stormwater Design*: Since the project team has decided to use native and adapted vegetation to meet requirements for WE Credit 1, the vegetation can also be used to achieve SS Credit 6. Native and adapted vegetation can reduce and treat stormwater runoff by increasing on-site infiltration, eliminating sources of contaminants, removing pollutants, and reducing impervious surfaces.

3. *SS Credit 7, Heat Island Effect*: The native and adapted vegetation used to meet requirements for WE Credit 1 can also be used to reduce the heat island effect on the project's roof and non-roof surfaces. The landscaped areas help to minimize the negative impact the heat island effect has on microclimates and on human and wildlife habitats.

Energy and Atmosphere

11. The project scenario indicates that the project will not perform an energy model. Energy models are useful because they can document compliance with energy codes. However, when an energy model is not used, a project team can still document EA Prerequisite 2, Minimum Energy Performance by submitting the following two ASHRAE/IESNA 90.1-2004 compliance forms.

- *mandatory measures form*: This form is applicable for all projects. The form includes mandatory provisions checklists for the building envelope, HVAC, service water heating, and lighting.

- *prescriptive requirements form*: This form is applicable only to projects using the prescriptive compliance approach. The form includes compliance documentation for the building envelope, HVAC, and service water heating.

12. EA Credit 1, Optimize Energy Performance, Option 2 is a prescriptive compliance path worth four points. This option requires a project team to comply with the prescriptive measures described in ASHRAE's *Advanced Energy Design Guide for Small Office Buildings 2004*. This compliance path includes recommendations for roofs, walls, floors, slabs, doors, vertical glazing, skylights, interior lighting, ventilation, ducts, energy recovery, and service water heating. The following restrictions apply to Option 2.

    • The building must be less than 20,000 sq ft.

    • The building must be office occupancy.

    • Project teams must comply with all applicable criteria as described in ASHRAE's *Advanced Energy Design Guide for Small Office Buildings 2004* for the building's appropriate climate zone. (There are eight climate zones in the United States.)

    Given the information in the project scenario, the project team will not achieve EA Credit 1 by using Option 2, because the building is greater than 20,000 sq ft and will be used primarily as a manufacturing facility, not an office space.

13. Waste energy recovery is applicable to EA Credit 1, Optimize Energy Performance via Option 1. Waste energy recovery is an energy efficiency technique that increases a building's energy performance by decreasing its energy consumption.

    However, in order to achieve EA Credit 1 via Option 1, a whole building energy simulation must be completed to demonstrate a percentage improvement in a building's performance rating. Points are awarded incrementally for increases in energy efficiency. The project scenario states that the project team will not complete an energy model; therefore, this project cannot earn points for EA Credit 1.

    (Note that waste energy recovery is often confused and falsely categorized as a source of on-site renewable energy. While waste energy recovery does decrease energy consumption, it does not create energy. Therefore, it is not an on-site renewable energy source and will not be applicable to EA Credit 2, On-Site Renewable Energy.)

14. EA Credit 1, Optimize Energy Performance, Option 4 is a prescriptive compliance path worth one point that requires a project to comply with the basic criteria and prescriptive measures of the Advanced Buildings Benchmark™ version 1.1. The project team must comply with all criteria stated in the Advanced Buildings Benchmark as defined by the project site's appropriate climate zone. Option 3 is applicable as there are no limitations on building type or size.

    (Note that the USGBC does not require compliance for the following sections of Advanced Buildings Benchmark version 1.1: Sec. 1.7 Monitoring and Trend-Logging; Sec. 1.11 Indoor Air Quality; and Sec. 1.14 Networked Computer Monitor Control.)

15. The USGBC considers the following materials renewable energy bio-fuels and eligible for EA Credit 2, On-Site Renewable Energy: untreated wood wastes, including mill residues; agricultural crops or waste; animal waste and other organic wastes; and landfill gas.

Materials not considered eligible for EA Credit 2 include municipal solid waste; forestry biomass waste, except mill residue; wood coated with paint; plastics or Formica™; wood treated for preservation; and materials containing halogens, chlorine compounds, halide compounds, chromatic copper arsenate, or arsenic. The USGBC states that if more than 1% of the wood fuel has been treated with these compounds, the energy system will be ineligible for EA Credit 2.

16. According to the USGBC, a basis of design (BOD) includes all information necessary to accomplish the owners' project requirements. Requirements include weather data; interior environmental criteria; pertinent design assumptions; cost goals; and references to applicable codes, standards, regulations, and guidelines.

    The commissioning authority must review the BOD prior to mid-construction documents. It must verify that the report adequately addresses all requirements, confirm that the design documents achieve the BOD goals, and coordinate with the commissioned systems. The commissioning authority must also review submittals for commissioned systems for compliance with the BOD. The final version of the BOD must be included in the Systems Manual developed by the commissioning authority.

17. EA Credit 4, Enhanced Refrigerant Management affects the design of the HVAC&R equipment by either prohibiting the use of refrigerants, or setting a maximum threshold for the combined contribution of ozone depletion and global warming potential of refrigerants. If the project design team completely eliminates the use of mechanical cooling and refrigeration equipment in the manufacturing facility, it will earn a point for EA Credit 4 because no refrigerants will be used. If the project requires a fire suppression system, the system cannot contain HCFCs or halons. Furthermore, no calculations or analysis are required if the project does not use refrigerants.

18. Because an energy model was not performed to provide the project's electrical consumption, the project team must use the Department of Energy Commercial Buildings Energy Consumption Survey database to determine the estimated electrical use. According to the *LEED-NC Reference Guide*, the median electrical intensity for an office is 11.7 kWh/ft²-yr. Since manufacturing is not listed, it can be classified as "other," which has an electrical intensity of 13.8 kWh/ft²-yr. The following calculations are used to determine the amount of green power this project must purchase to achieve EA Credit 6, Green Power.

    The office annual electrical consumption is

    $$\text{office consumption} = (40{,}000 \text{ ft}^2)\left(11.7 \frac{\text{kWh}}{\frac{\text{ft}^2}{\text{yr}}}\right)$$

    $$= 468{,}000 \text{ kWh/yr}$$

    The "other" annual electrical consumption is

    $$\text{other consumption} = (36{,}000 \text{ ft}^2)\left(13.8 \frac{\text{kWh}}{\frac{\text{ft}^2}{\text{yr}}}\right)$$

    $$= 496{,}800 \text{ kWh/yr}$$

Add the office and the "other" electrical consumption to find the total annual electrical consumption.

$$\text{total annual consumption} = 468{,}000 \; \frac{\text{kWh}}{\text{yr}} + 496{,}800 \; \frac{\text{kWh}}{\text{yr}}$$

$$= 964{,}800 \; \text{kWh/yr}$$

Then, find the required annual green power.

$$\text{green annual power} = 35\% \times (\text{total annual})(2 \; \text{yr})$$

$$= (0.35)\left(964{,}800 \; \frac{\text{kWh}}{\text{yr}}\right)(2 \; \text{yr})$$

$$= 675{,}360 \; \text{kWh}$$

The project must purchase 675,360 kWh of green power annually, for a minimum time period of two years.

Materials and Resources

19. This project *does* qualify for MR Credit 1, Building Reuse. The project scenario indicates that the existing building is 36,000 sq ft and the addition is 40,000 sq ft.

MR Credit 1 stipulates for projects that include an addition to an existing building, the square footage of the addition cannot be more than two times the square footage of the existing building. Based on the square footage of this project, the addition can be up to 72,000 sq ft and still earn points for MR Credit 1.

20. The following items must be excluded from calculations for MR Credit 1.1 and MR Credit 1.2, Building Reuse:

a. non-structural roofing materials

b. window assemblies

c. structural and envelope materials that are deemed to be structurally unsound

d. structural and envelope materials that are considered hazardous and pose a contamination risk to building occupants

21. This project *will* qualify for MR Credit 1.3, Maintain 50% of Interior Non-Structural Elements. Projects are not required to achieve MR Credit 1.1 or 1.2 to be considered for MR Credit 1.3, as neither MR Credit 1.1 nor 1.2 verifies the requirements of MR Credit 1.3. MR Credit 1.1 and 1.2 are separate calculations based on structural building components.

22. To calculate the area of reused materials for MR Credit 1.3, Building Reuse: Maintain 50% of Interior Non-Structural Elements, use the following guidelines.

    a. Finished ceilings and flooring are calculated as areas including one side of the material.

    b. For interior non-structural walls, determine the finished area between floor and ceiling and multipy by two. (Both sides of interior non-structural walls are included in the calculations.)

    c. The surface areas of interior doors are calculated including one side of the door.

    d. Calculate the interior casework using the visible surface area of the assembly.

23. MR Credit 2, Construction Waste Management offers points to projects that divert at least 50% of construction or demolition debris from a landfill or incinerator. Since this project achieved MR Credit 1.1, it cannot apply the reused existing building materials to achieve MR Credit 2. If the addition was more than two times the size of the existing building, and therefore could not earn credit for MR Credit 1, Building Reuse, then the project could earn points for MR Credit 2 because it would be diverting this waste from a landfill.

This project is also unable to achieve MR Credit 3, Materials Reuse, because salvaged or recycled materials that are used to qualify for MR Credits 1, 2, 4, 6, or 7 cannot also qualify for MR Credit 3. Additionally, for projects wishing to achieve MR Credit 3, reused existing building materials must meet the following conditions.

    • *fixed components*: Materials that are no longer able to serve their original function must be reconditioned for a different use or installed in a different location.

    • *finished materials*: Materials may continue to serve their original function, but must undergo refurbishment to become functional.

24. The removal of contaminated soil does *not* contribute to MR Credit 2, Construction Waste Management. Although these materials were diverted from the landfill, according to the *LEED-NC Reference Guide*, hazardous waste and excavated soils are to be excluded from these calculations.

25. A total waste diversion rate of 95% or greater is required to earn an Innovation in Design point for MR Credit 2, Construction Waste Management. Calculations may be based on either weight or volume, but must be consistent throughout project documentation.

26. The value of rapidly renewable materials is calculated based on a percentage of rapidly renewable materials to the overall materials cost of the project for divisions 2–10. The total value of materials used on the project can be provided by the general contractor based on actual costs. The total value of materials used on the project can also be calculated as 45% of the construction costs. Actual costs of rapidly renewable material are the materials only cost to the job, which excludes all labor, overhead, profit, rental fees, and so forth.

Since the materials cost is unknown, calculate it from the construction cost provided with the project information.

$$\text{total materials cost (for divisions 2-10)} = (45\%)\left(\text{overall construction cost (for divisions 2-10)}\right)$$

$$= (0.45)(\$11,400,000)$$

$$= \$5,130,000$$

The percent value of rapidly renewable materials is based on the following formula.

$$\% \text{ rapidly renewable materials} = \frac{\text{cost of rapidly renewable materials}}{\text{total materials cost (for divisions 2-10)}}$$

In order to earn one point for MR Credit 6, 2.5% of the materials must be rapidly renewable materials and products. Use the previous formula to find the cost of rapidly renewable materials.

$$2.5\% = \frac{\text{cost of rapidly renewable materials}}{\$5,130,000}$$

$$\text{cost of rapidly renewable materials} = (0.025)(\$5,130,000)$$

$$= \$128,250$$

$128,250 is the minimum dollar value of rapidly renewable materials necessary to earn a point for MR Credit 6.

Indoor Environmental Quality

27. Because the manufacturing facility is non-residential and the project design will include an indoor smoking area for its employees, the project team must comply with the requirements of EQ Prerequisite 2, Environmental Tobacco Smoke (ETS) Control, Option 2. Smoking must be prohibited in the building except in the designated smoking area. The design must provide the designated smoking area with negative pressure, which will prevent contaminated air from flowing out of the designated smoking area. A separate ventilation system must also be installed and tested under worst-case conditions as specified by the *LEED-NC Reference Guide* to ensure that the system is capable of generating the required negative pressure. Any exterior smoking areas must be a minimum of 25 ft away from entries, outdoor air intakes, and operable windows.

28. EQ Credit 2, Increased Ventilation requires that mechanical ventilation systems increase the outdoor air ventilation rates by a minimum of 30% above the rates specified by ASHRAE 62.1-2004. Increasing the outdoor air ventilation rates will have a negative impact on the energy consumption of the building, as it may increase fan use, which consumes energy. Furthermore, the additional outdoor air will likely need to be conditioned at certain points throughout the year. This conditioning might entail heating, cooling, humidifying, or dehumidifying the air.

However, increasing the outdoor air ventilation rates also increases the quantity of fresh outdoor air in the building to improve the comfort, well-being, and productivity of the employees. This juxtaposition of increased energy consumption and improved occupant comfort is known as a trade-off, where one green building strategy has a negative impact on another green building strategy.

It is important to analyze the social and economic benefits related to health and productivity due to increased ventilation. Then weigh these benefits against the environmental and economic benefits due to reduced energy consumption.

29. The referenced standard for EQ Credit 4.1, Low-Emitting Materials: Adhesives and Sealants is the South Coast Air Quality Management District (SCAQMD) Rule #1168. This standard requires that all rubber floor adhesives have a volatile organic compound (VOC) limit of 60 g/L less water and exempt compounds. The problem stated that the VOC content for the adhesive used in the site's rubber flooring was 65 g/L. Therefore, the adhesive does not meet the requirements for this credit.

30. The LEED-NC Rating System provides the following maximum volatile organic compound (VOC) limits for EQ Credit 4.2, Low-Emitting Materials: Paints and Coatings.

    a. architectural paints, flats: 50 g/L

    b. architectural paints, non-flats: 150 g/L

    c. anti-rust paints: 250 g/L

    d. wood stains: 250 g/L

    e. exterior wood stains: There are no requirements for exterior coatings and paints.

31. The following three systems must be documented to comply with EQ Credit 4.3, Low-Emitting Materials: Carpets Systems, along with their referenced standards, in order to earn a point for this credit.

    a. *carpet*: All interior carpet must be listed in, and comply with, the standards of the Carpet and Rug Institute's Green Label Plus Program.

    b. *carpet cushions*: All interior carpet cushions must be listed in, and comply with, the standards of the Carpet and Rug Institute's Green Label Program.

    c. *carpet adhesives*: All carpet adhesives must comply with the requirements of EQ Credit 4.1, Low-Emitting Materials: Adhesives and Sealants, which references South Coast Air Quality Management District (SCAQMD) Rule #1168. For carpet adhesives, this standard indicates a maximum VOC limit of 50 g/L.

32. To earn points for EQ Credit 7.1, Thermal Comfort: Design, during the project's planning and design phase, the project team must identify the desired thermal comfort ranges for the building occupants and the environmental parameters for the building. The project team is encouraged to collaborate with the owners to establish these parameters. Variables that impact these decisions include project size, program, location, regional climate, and type of occupancy. From this data, the project team must determine whether to move forward with a passive or an active conditioning system for the building.

33. One HVAC system strategy that would provide the owner-desired level of control to the building occupants and that complies with EQ Credit 6.2, Controllability of Systems: Thermal Comfort is the use of an under-floor air distribution system. This flexible system allows for individual thermal comfort control through in-floor or desk-mounted air diffusers. Conventional ceiling-mounted air diffusers used in conjunction with individually controlled variable air volume (VAV) boxes would also meet both requirements. Other possible thermal comfort control strategies include individual thermostats for occupants, operable windows, individual radiant panels, or a combination of these strategies.

34. If in 6 to 18 months after occupancy, more than 20% of the building's occupants are dissatisfied with the level of thermal comfort, the project team should complete a Plan for Corrective Action. Corrective actions should be based on ASHRAE Standard 55 and may include, but are not limited to, control adjustments (e.g., temperature set points, schedules, operating modes), diffuser airflow adjustments, and solar control.

Innovation and Design Process

Note: The following Innovation and Design Process solutions are based on hypothetical project scenarios and were derived from researching past Innovation in Design Credit Interpretation Rulings. These suggested innovations have not been formally submitted to the USGBC for approval. Therefore, if pursuing any of the following innovations, it is recommended one research current Innovation in Design Credit Interpretation Rulings, or submit Credit Interpretation Requests to the USGBC.

35. ID Credit 1, Innovation in Design for Exemplary Performance, provides design teams the opportunity to be awarded points for exceptional performance above the requirements set by the LEED-NC Rating System. Exemplary performance ID credits are generally awarded for doubling the credit requirements and/or achieving the next incremental percentage threshold. Based on the project scenario, the following options provide two potential opportunities to achieve ID Credit 1.

Option 1—MR Credit 4, Recycled Content—Exemplary Performance: The project scenario provides information that indicates a strong effort will be made to select materials with recycled content. The project will try and exceed the baseline for MR Credit 4, Recycled Content criteria, which is 20%, and achieve the threshold established by the LEED-NC Rating System, which is 30%.

Option 2—MR Credit 5, Regional Materials—Exemplary Performance: The project scenario provides information that indicates a strong effort will be made to select materials that are local. The project will try to exceed the baseline for MR Credit 5, Regional Materials criteria, which is 20%, and achieve the threshold established by LEED-NC Rating System, which is 40%.

36. ID Credit 1, Innovation in Design for Innovative Performance, provides design teams the opportunity to be awarded points for innovative performance outside of the requirements set by the LEED-NC Rating System. Innovative performance ID credits are generally awarded for comprehensive strategies that demonstrate significant and quantifiable environmental and/or health benefits. Based on the project scenario, the following options are two potential opportunities to achieve ID Credit 1.

Option 1—Non-Cementitous Mix—Innovative Performance: The project team will submit documentation that the concrete used on site was from a reduced cementitious mix. This green building strategy greatly reduces the negative impact that the mining of concrete mixing agents has on the environment. The project will require 15%

flyash and 25% slag in all concrete mixes used on site as approved by the structural engineer. This will be compared with local standards in concrete mixes.

Option 2—Heat Recovery from Process Loads—Innovative Performance: Process loads are not regulated in the LEED-NC Rating System or in ASHRAE standards. This project plans to use process heat-recovery systems to preheat process water and to provide heating to the building when necessary. Calculations must document the reduction of energy consumption as a quantifiable environmental benefit.

Public Library Problems

4

Vicinity Plan

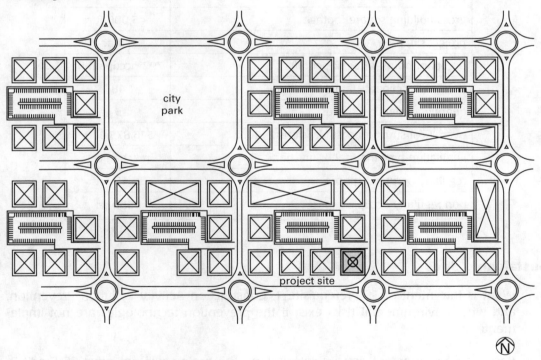

Scenario

A new public library will be constructed for the city of Emberville, North Carolina, on a site that is currently an asphalt parking lot. The city has identified the following list of priorities for this project:

- revitalize the downtown area
- provide a comfortable, daylit public space

- incorporate space for a children's center

- use solar energy (photovoltaics) for 25% of power requirements

- minimize interior and exterior potable water consumption by using rainwater cisterns and a greywater system

- maximize indoor air quality

- reduce toxins in the selection of materials

- incorporate reused and recycled materials

- demonstrate a commitment to the community and the environment through public education about the project's use of green building techniques and strategies

The city has determined that the project may use the steel from a nearby existing bridge that is no longer in use and scheduled for demolition. Though Emberville has no commuter rail, the library will be linked to other public transportation. The available parking in the downtown area should nearly meet the new library's parking demands.

General Information	
project building footprint	26,300 ft²
gross building square footage	45,000 ft²
project site area	0.3 ac
occupant hours (at peak period)	792 occupant-hr
transient occupants (at peak period)	48
quantity of parking spaces	5
overall construction cost (divisions 2–10)	$16,875,000
ventilation type (natural or mechanical)	mechanical
regularly occupied spaces	36,450 ft²
non-regularly occupied spaces	8550 ft²

Sustainable Sites

1. What is the intent of SS Prerequisite 1, Construction Activity Pollution Prevention, and what environmental risks exist if the prevention technologies are not implemented?

2. Based on development density calculations, the project will not meet SS Credit 2, Development Density and Community Connectivity, Option 1. What project documentation is required to meet Option 2?

3. Which of the two options for SS Credit 4.1, Alternative Transportation: Public Transportation Access is most appropriate and how should project compliance be documented?

4. Which option for SS Credit 6.1, Stormwater Design: Quantity Control is most appropriate and how should project compliance be documented?

5. According to SS Credit 6.2, Stormwater Design: Quality Control, are the stormwater management measures for this project considered nonstructural or structural measures? Why is this significant?

6. How is SRI related to SS Credit 7.1, Heat Island Effect: Non-Roof? How does SRI affect a building's performance? How does it differ from infrared emittance?

Water Efficiency

7. The library will demonstrate water conservation to the public through interpretive signage and exhibits. The city of Emberville would like to use a variety of water conservation strategies to accomplish this task. What green building strategies can be employed to achieve WE Credit 1, Water Efficient Landscaping? List and explain four.

8. Based on the following information, confirm which credits in WE Credit 1, Water Efficient Landscaping this project will achieve and explain why. Data is representative of July conditions. LEED specifies July because it is typically the month with the greatest evapotranspiration effects and therefore has the greatest irrigation demands.

- The baseline case calculates that the total water applied ($TWA_{baseline}$) is 122,500 gal.
- The design case total water applied ($TWA_{design\ case}$) is 33,400 gal.
- The design case water reuse contribution ($Reuse_{design\ case}$) is 3900 gal of water from the rainwater catchment system.

9. WE Credit 3.1, Water Use Reduction: 20% Reduction calculations are based on the use of interior water fixtures and the number of building occupants. Calculate the full-time equivalent (FTE) of building occupants and the transient occupants, and determine the gender ratio for the project.

Energy and Atmosphere

10. The city will hire a commissioning authority in order to comply with EA Prerequisite 1, Fundamental Commissioning of the Building Energy Systems. Based on square footage, what qualifications must the commissioning authority have?

11. Who must submit documentation for EA Prerequisite 3, Fundamental Refrigerant Management? Also, what documentation is required and during what stage must it be submitted?

12. The landscape architect is proposing to plant a row of deciduous trees along the south and west sidewalks adjacent to the building in order to meet SS Credit 7.1, Non-Roof. Is this a synergy or trade-off with EA Credit 1, Optimize Energy Performance? Explain.

13. Pending budget approval, the design team would like to pursue Option 1 for EA Credit 1, Optimize Energy Performance. Option 1 is worth up to 10 points and requires an energy simulation using the performance rating method. Explain how to calculate the percentage improvement for EA Credit 1, Option 1 based on the results of the whole building energy simulation.

14. The project will meet the requirements for EA Prerequisite 1, Fundamental Commissioning of the Building Energy Systems, with an independent, third-party commissioning authority hired directly by the city. What additional tasks will this commissioning authority need to complete in order to obtain a point for EA Credit 3, Enhanced Commissioning?

15. The intent of EA Credit 4, Enhanced Refrigerant Management is to reduce ozone depletion and minimize direct contributions to global warming. What compounds contribute to ozone depletion and global warming? Where are they found? How do they deplete the ozone and/or contribute to global warming?

16. Assuming the budget for the project was approved to include a whole building energy simulation for EA Credit 1, Optimize Energy Performance, which option for International Performance Measurement and Verification Protocol (IPMVP) Volume III is most appropriate for the documentation of EA Credit 5, Measurement and Verification (M&V)? What must be included in the M&V plan under this option?

Materials and Resources

17. More than 80% of the library waste stream consists of corrugated cardboard. Given this, does the project site require facilities for the recycling of other materials per MR Prerequisite 1, Storage and Collection of Recyclables? Explain.

18. The project's construction manager is gathering data and specifications for the construction waste management plan. In order to document MR Credit 2, Construction Waste Management, should the amount of waste be determined by weight or by volume?

19. The general contractor has communicated to the city that construction waste management adds cost due to on-site recycling requirements. The construction company has asked to be compensated for these added costs. The project's LEED AP wants to present the contractor with a list of ways these costs are offset by the construction waste management being used. Describe how the waste management costs are offset.

20. The project architect has planned on using an existing bridge as a source of structural steel. The steel will need to be sandblasted and possibly painted to remove and/or seal any lead paint that was used in the original installation. The bridge is located about 180 mi from the project site. Explain which credit the reuse of the bridge steel applies to: MR Credit 3, Materials Reuse, or MR Credit 5, Regional Materials.

21. The project team is evaluating the use of FSC-certified wood for the project. The architect estimates that the majority of the wood used on the project will be plywood. A ¾ in plywood backer, to be installed throughout the stacks area, will account for 52% of the wood used in the library. This value is based on square footage of materials with similar thickness. The 1 in × 4 in wood paneling used for the ceiling in the lobby, research, and circulation areas is the library's other major wood element in the building (39%). The architect has determined that the cost difference between plywood and certified plywood is not prohibitive and has assumed that compliance with MR Credit 7, Certified Wood can be determined by the square footage of materials with similar thicknesses. Is the architect's assumption correct?

22. The project team wants to earn two points for MR Credit 3, Materials Reuse. Explain how the value of salvaged materials is calculated. Based on the 45% default materials value, what is the minimum dollar amount of reuse materials necessary for the project to earn 2 points for MR Credit 3?

23. The city will supply the library's office furniture, which will contain recycled content. Can the project team apply the furniture's recycled content toward MR Credit 4, Recycled Content?

24. The project team is deciding on the best allocation of the materials budget. They are considering credits and synergies related to rapidly renewable materials. How does the USGBC define rapidly renewable building materials? List at least four examples of rapidly renewable building materials.

Indoor Environmental Quality

25. The city of Emberville prohibits smoking in all public buildings. What must be documented to comply with EQ Prerequisite 2, Environmental Tobacco Smoke (ETS) Control?

26. What are three types of basic methods for ventilating buildings?

27. The project wants to earn EQ Credit 3.1, Construction IAQ Management Plan: During Construction. This credit references the Sheet Metal and Air Conditioning Contractors' of North America (SMACNA) IAQ Guidelines for Occupied Buildings Under Construction. These guidelines recommend what five areas for control measures? How does each area improve the building's indoor air quality for the construction team during construction?

28. The project team is gathering documentation for the Design Submittal to USGBC. The team is planning to submit documentation for EQ Credit 4.1, Low-Emitting Materials: Adhesives and Sealants. Is it appropriate to submit documentation for EQ Credit 4.1 at this phase of the process? Why or why not?

29. The project team is working to create a high quality indoor environment. In order to achieve this, one strategy is to comply with EQ Credit 4.4, Low-Emitting Materials: Composite Wood and Agrifiber Products. What types of products does this credit refer to? What must be provided to document this credit?

30. The project team is documenting compliance with EQ Credit 5, Indoor Chemical and Pollutant Source Control. One requirement is for chemical storage rooms to have a dedicated exhaust system. Explain what a dedicated exhaust system entails relative to the scope of the LEED-NC Rating System.

31. The project's lighting designer wants to comply with EQ Credit 6.1, Controllability of Systems: Lighting. The lighting designer is trying to provide 90% of the individuals with control over their lighting systems, but is challenged by the library's open public spaces. Determine the best approach to control the lighting for this type of occupancy while complying with EQ Credit 6.1.

32. Complete the following spreadsheet to provide documentation for EQ Credit 8.2, Daylight and Views: Views for 90% of Spaces. Based on the information provided, determine the appropriate view areas in square feet to be included in the credit's calculations.

room	occupied floor area (ft²)	plan area of direct line of sight to perimeter visionglazing (ft²)	calculated area of direct line of sight to vision glazing (ft²)	horizontal view at 42" AFF (YES or NO)	compliant area (ft²)
private office 100	180	138		YES	
private office 101	170	125		YES	
private office 102	180	160		YES	
copy room 103	135	120		YES	
restrooms 104 and 105	410	0		NO	
private office 106	180	132		NO	
open office 107	2340	2270		YES	
open office 108	1370	1260		YES	
total (ft²)					
percent of view areas					

Innovation and Design Process

33. List two potential exemplary performance strategies based on the project scenario. Explain how each meets requirements for ID Credit 1, Innovation in Design for Exemplary Performance.

34. List two potential innovative performance strategies based on the project scenario. Explain how each meets requirements for ID Credit 1, Innovation in Design for Innovative Strategies.

Public Library Solutions

Sustainable Sites

1. The intent of SS Prerequisite 1, Construction Activity Pollution Prevention is to reduce pollution from construction activities by controlling soil erosion, waterway sedimentation, and airborne dust generation.

   If construction activity pollution is not prevented, the environmental risks include erosion, sedimentation, and airborne dust generation. Topsoil erosion reduces the soil's ability to support plant life, regulate water absorption, and maintain biodiversity. Sedimentation in water channels lowers oxygen levels, consequently reducing aquatic life. Sedimentation also lessens flow capacity, thus increasing flooding potential. Airborne dust generation can cause both health and industrial problems such as occupational respiratory diseases and damage to equipment.

2. To meet Option 2 (Community Connectivity) of SS Credit 2, the project must prepare a site map marked with a minimum number of relevant sites within a half-mile radius of the main building entrance. Relevant sites include at least one area zoned for a residential development with at least 10 units per acre, and at least 10 commercial service buildings with pedestrian access between the service and the project.

3. SS Credit 4.1, Alternative Transportation: Public Transportation Access can be achieved by two options. Option 1 requires the project's location to be within a half mile of an existing (or planned and funded) commuter rail, light rail, or subway station. Option 2 requires a project's location to be within a quarter mile of one or more stops for two or more public or campus bus lines usable by building occupants.

   The project statement clearly states that Emberville does not have a commuter rail, but that other public transportation is nearby, so Option 2 is most appropriate. Project compliance should be documented by providing a site map showing the existing bus stops and lines serviced within a quarter mile of the project. It is also helpful to include a list of other bus stops in the area, the lines they service, and their distance from the project's site in miles.

4. SS Credit 6.1, Stormwater Design: Quantity Control, Option 1 applies to sites with an existing imperviousness of less than or equal to 50%. These are generally undeveloped or lightly developed sites. Option 2 applies to largely developed sites with an existing imperviousness greater than 50%. Based on the project description and site map shown, Option 2 is most appropriate.

The following measurements are required to document compliance with SS Credit 6.1, Option 2:

- pre-development site runoff rate (cfs)
- pre-development site runoff quantity (cf)
- post-development site runoff rate (cfs)
- post-development site runoff quantity (cf)

To earn SS Credit 6.1, Option 2, the post-development rate and quantity must be at least 25% less than the respective pre-development values.

5. The only stormwater management measure mentioned in the project statement is the use of rainwater cisterns, which is considered a structural measure. Structural measures are preferred on urban constrained sites with significant imperviousness because they require minimal space allocation and land use. Structural measures include cisterns, manhole treatment devices, ponds, and subsurface stormwater filters.

The selection of structural versus nonstructural stormwater management measures is significant because the documentation requirements are based on the type of control measure. To earn this credit, structural measures must have the capacity to treat at least 90% of the annual rainfall volume.

6. SRI is the solar reflectance index. It is a measure of a material's ability to reject solar heat and is a calculated combination of a material's solar spectrum reflectivity and emissivity. Materials that have a low SRI value, such as black asphalt, absorb solar heat and increase the heat island effect. A standard black color has a reflectance of 0.05, an emittance of 0.90, and an SRI of 0. Materials that have a high SRI value, such as light-colored concrete, reflect solar heat and decrease the heat island effect. A standard white color has a reflectance of 0.80, an emittance of 0.90, and an SRI of 100.

A building's energy consumption and regional air quality is affected by the SRIs of the site surface and roofing materials. Materials with high SRIs decrease a building's demand for cooling, while those with low SRIs increase the demand for cooling. In warm climates or warm seasons, the heat island effect increases the energy load on a building because of the higher temperatures in the areas immediately surrounding the building.

Pavement and other ground surfaces with high SRIs increase the quality of the nighttime visual environment. Therefore, exterior site lighting systems can use less energy.

Infrared emittance, or emissivity, measures a material's ability to shed heat in the form of infrared radiation.

SRI has a scale of 0 to 100 and infrared emittance has a scale of 0 to 1. In both scales, higher measurements represent a greater reduction in the heat island effect.

Water Efficiency

7. The library can employ the following four green building strategies to earn WE Credit 1, Water Efficient Landscaping.

- *High-efficiency irrigation systems,* such as a micro-irrigation system or irrigation controllers. Micro-irrigation systems slowly add water at the plant's roots (rather than on the surface of the soil), which allows for more saturation and less runoff and evaporation.

- *Irrigation controllers* monitor environmental conditions, ensuring that watering takes place only when necessary. Less potable water is used and plants are not over-irrigated. Moisture sensors, rain shut-offs, and weather-based evapotranspiration controllers are all types of irrigation controllers.

- *Greywater systems* can reduce the amount of potable water used to irrigate the landscape. These systems collect rainwater and/or capture domestic wastewater that has not come in contact with blackwater. There is no commonly accepted definition for blackwater so it is best to check with the local authority having jurisdiction. However, blackwater sources always include wastewater from toilets and urinals. Other sources may include wastewater from kitchen sinks, showers, or bathtubs. If used to irrigate landscaping, a greywater system can help earn WE Credit 1. The system can also be used for interior non-potable water purposes.

- *Appropriate landscaping* can greatly decrease water consumption. Native or adapted plants require minimal irrigation and can maximize regional environmental conditions. Mulching, groundcover, and soil amendments also reduce irrigation demand by decreasing evaporation and runoff. Typically, projects need to minimize turf areas, which often use non-native species and require intensive irrigation.

8. For the project to meet the requirements of WE Credit 1.1, Water Efficient Landscaping: Reduce by 50%, there must be at least a 50% reduction of potable water use through high-efficiency irrigation technology, or the use of greywater. To meet the requirements of WE Credit 1.2, Water Efficient Landscaping: No Potable Use or No Irrigation, the project's landscaping must either use 100% greywater, or not require the installation of a permanent irrigation system.

Using the given baseline and design case values for July (the month with the highest irrigation demand), calculate the project's potable water reduction.

$$TPWA_{design\ case} = TWA_{design\ case} - Reuse_{design\ case}$$

$$= 33{,}400\ gal - 3900\ gal$$

$$= 29{,}500\ gal$$

$$\%\ reduction\ of\ potable\ water = \left(1 - \frac{TPWA_{design\ case}}{TWA_{baseline}}\right) \times 100\%$$

$$= \left(1 - \frac{29{,}500\ gal}{122{,}500\ gal}\right) \times 100\%$$

$$= 75.9\%$$

$$\% \text{ reduction of total water} = \left(1 - \frac{TWA_{\text{design case}}}{TWA_{\text{baseline}}}\right) \times 100\%$$

$$= \left(1 - \frac{33{,}400 \text{ gal}}{122{,}500 \text{ gal}}\right) \times 100\%$$

$$= 72.7\%$$

Based on these calculations, the project will meet the requirements for WE Credit 1.1.

9. The full-time equivalent for building occupants is determined by dividing the occupant hours by eight hours, which represents the average work day.

$$\text{FTE occupants} = \frac{\text{occupant hours}}{8 \text{ hr}}$$

$$= \frac{792 \text{ occupant-hr}}{8 \text{ hr}}$$

$$= 99 \text{ occupants}$$

$$\text{transient occupants} = \text{estimated representative daily average}$$

$$= 48 \text{ occupants (given in general information table)}$$

Note that in the baseline and design case interior water use calculations for WE Credit 3, Water Use Reduction, the total annual volume of water used must be calculated independently for full-time equivalent and transient occupants.

USGBC LEED-NC standards require a consistent and balanced, one-to-one gender ratio unless specific project conditions warrant an alternative. The gender ratio for the project is assumed to be one-to-one.

Energy and Atmosphere

10. For projects smaller than 50,000 sq ft, the commissioning authority must have documented commissioning authority experience in at least two projects of similar managerial and technical complexity. The commissioning authority may be any of the following: a qualified person on the design or construction team, an employee of the design or construction management, a qualified employee of the owner, or a consultant of the owner.

11. The mechanical engineer will need to use the LEED-Online template to submit documentation confirming the project does not use CFC refrigerants in the base building HVAC&R systems. This must be submitted in the design submittal phase.

12. Proposing to plant a row of deciduous trees along the south and west sidewalks adjacent to the building is a synergy between SS Credit 7.1, Non-Roof and EA Credit 1, Optimize Energy Performance. In the context of the LEED-NC Rating System, a synergy is a green building strategy that, when applied, contributes to the achievement of more than one LEED credit.

The deciduous trees create a synergy in two ways: they will shade the sidewalks during warm months, which will reduce the site's heat island effect, and they will reduce the solar heat gain emitted through the south and west building windows.

13. To qualify for EA Credit 1, the project team must run a minimum of five energy simulations. These five simulations consist of one proposed design simulation and four baseline design simulations. The four baseline simulations consist of the building modeled with minimum ASHRAE 90.1-2004 standards with four different building orientations (each one rotated 90°). The average of the total projected annual energy costs for the four baseline design simulations is used as a reference for the baseline building performance. This average is necessary to calculate the percentage improvement over the baseline building performance.

    Percentage improvement is calculated by the following equation.

    $$\text{percentage improvement} = 100\% - \frac{\text{proposed building performance}}{\text{baseline building performance}}$$

14. To earn an additional point for EA Credit 3, Enhanced Commissioning, the commissioning authority must complete the following tasks.

    - conduct a commissioning design review prior to mid-construction documents

    - review contractor submittals applicable to systems being commissioned

    - collaborate with the project team to develop a systems manual for the commissioned systems

    - verify completion of training requirements with the project team

    - review building operation within 10 months after substantial completion

15. Compounds that contribute to ozone depletion include chlorofluorocarbons (CFCs) and hydrochlorofluorocarbons (HCFCs). Compounds that contribute to global warming include, but are not limited to CFCs, HCFCs, and hydrofluorocarbons (HFCs).

    These compounds are commonly used refrigerants found in building heating, ventilating, air conditioning, and refrigeration (HVAC&R) equipment. Common building applications of CFCs are chillers, refrigerators, dehumidifiers, and fire suppression systems. Common applications of HCFCs are air conditioners, fire suppression systems, and the CFC replacement in chillers. HFCs are commonly found in refrigerators, air conditioners, and the insulation agent of chillers.

    CFCs and HCFCs contribute to both ozone depletion and global warming. HFCs do not contribute appreciably to ozone depletion, but do contribute to global warming. These compounds can leak into the environment during installation, operation, servicing, and decommissioning of the HVAC&R equipment.

16. The International Performance Measurement and Verification Protocol (IPMVP) Volume III provides four options for measurement and verification (M&V), two of which are recognized by the LEED-NC Rating System's EA Credit 5, Measurement and Verification. Option D, Whole Building Calibrated Simulation Savings Estimation, is the most appropriate for this project. It compares the actual energy use of the building to the performance predicted by the whole building energy simulation.

The requirements for the M&V plan under Option D are as follows.

- identify the IPMVP Volume III option to be applied
- define the baseline energy use
- identify metering requirements
- outline specific methodologies for implementing the chosen M&V plan

Materials and Resources

17. MR Prerequisite 1, Storage and Collection of Recyclables *does* require well marked collection and storage areas for recyclables, including (at a minimum) paper, corrugated cardboard, glass, plastic, and metals. However, the prerequisite does not reference quantities or percentages of recycled materials, only that the aforementioned materials have ample space for recycling.

18. The construction manager can determine the amount of construction waste either by weight or volume, as long as the value is used consistently in the calculations.

19. Though hiring a company to provide on-site construction waste management services does add service costs to a project, these costs are often offset by reduced tipping (i.e., waste disposal) fees. In many cases, the cost of recycling materials is less than the cost of disposing these materials in a landfill—especially as landfill capacity decreases and disposal costs and regulations increase. Additionally, recycling certain metals, such as aluminum or scrap metal, can generate revenue and avoid some tipping, or disposal, fees.

20. Reusing the bridge steel qualifies as a synergy as it contributes toward achieving *both* MR Credit 3, Materials Reuse and MR Credit 5, Regional Materials. MR Credit 3 provides points for the reuse of salvaged materials. Since the bridge steel was also extracted, manufactured, and/or processed within 500 mi of the project, using it also contributes to MR Credit 5.

In the context of the LEED-NC Rating System, a synergy is a green building strategy that, when applied, contributes to the achievement of more than one LEED credit.

21. The architect is *not* correct in assuming that that compliance with MR Credit 7, Certified Wood can be determined by the square footage of materials with similar thicknesses. The percentage of FSC certified wood on the project is calculated based on a dollar value of material cost (not the square footage or similar materials), using the following equation.

$$\% \text{ certified wood material} = \frac{\text{FSC-certified wood material value}}{\text{total new wood material value}}$$

All new wood on the project that is permanently installed must be included in the wood calculations. The type of wood that is exempt from these calculations is wood that is previously used, and wood used for framing, bracing, and other temporary uses.

22. The percentage of salvaged materials is calculated based on a comparison of the project's salvaged material costs to the overall material costs. The total value of materials used on the project can either be provided by the general contractor based on actual costs, or it can be a nominal 45% of the construction costs. Salvaged material costs include the cost of the material only—costs related to labor, overhead, profit, rental fees, transportation, and the like must be excluded.

For this project, actual material costs are not known, so the total value of materials can be calculated as 45% of the overall construction cost (for divisions 2–10).

$$\text{total materials cost (for divisions 2-10)} = (45\%)\left(\text{overall construction cost (for divisions 2-10)}\right)$$

$$= (0.45)(\$16{,}875{,}000)$$

$$= \$7{,}593{,}750$$

The percentage of salvaged, or reused, material is based on the cost of the reused materials divided by the total materials cost.

$$\%\text{ reuse materials} = \frac{\text{cost of reuse materials}}{\text{total materials cost}}$$

To earn two points in MR Credit 3, Materials Reuse, a minimum of 10% of the materials must be salvaged, refurbished, or reused on a cost basis.

$$10\%\text{ reuse materials} = \frac{\text{cost of reuse materials}}{\text{total materials cost}}$$

$$\text{cost of reuse materials} = (10\%)(\text{ total materials cost })$$

$$= (0.10)(\$7{,}593{,}750)$$

$$= \$759{,}375 \quad (\$760{,}000)$$

Approximately $760,000 must be spent on reused material to earn two points for MR Credit 3.

23. The project team can apply the value of recycled content of any furniture provided by the city, but only if this value is included consistently in calculations for MR Credits 3 through 7.

24. The USGBC defines rapidly renewable materials as "an agricultural product, both fiber and animal, that takes 10 years or less to grow or raise, and to harvest in an ongoing and sustainable fashion."

Some examples of rapidly renewable resources include cork, linoleum, wool, cotton, bamboo, small diameter trees, wheatboard, strawboard, and sunflower seeds.

Indoor Environmental Quality

25. The project team must document that smoking in the building is prohibited and that all exterior designated smoking areas are a minimum of 25 ft from entries, outdoors air intakes, and operable windows.

26. The three methods for ventilating buildings are active, passive, and mixed-mode. Active ventilation involves the use of mechanical systems. Passive ventilation uses natural ventilation. Mixed-mode ventilation uses both mechanical and natural ventilation methods.

27. The Sheet Metal and Air Conditioning Contractors' of North America (SMACNA) Guidelines recommends indoor air quality (IAQ) control measures in five areas: HVAC protection, source control, pathway interruption, housekeeping, and scheduling.

- HVAC protection prevents the HVAC systems from contamination by dust, debris, and odors during construction.

- Source control reduces, mitigates, and/or eliminates air contaminants by careful selection of low-emitting products. It is a synergy with EQ Credit 4, Low-Emitting Materials.

- Pathway interruption stops the movement of contaminated air from construction areas to occupied spaces by isolating or compartmentalizing construction areas.

- Housekeeping refers to the prompt cleanup of dust, spills, and moisture created in the construction process. These practices help control the release of airborne particles and contaminants into the indoor air.

- Proper scheduling allows highly polluting activities to be conducted during off-hours, allows time for off-gassing, and reduces the exposure of construction workers and building occupants to pollutants.

28. Documentation for EQ Credit 4.1, Low-Emitting Materials: Adhesives and Sealants should be submitted as part of the construction submittal, not the design submittal. To meet the credit requirements, the project team must verify which adhesives and sealants were used and installed during construction; therefore, documentation cannot be submitted prior to construction completion.

29. The types of products that EQ Credit 4.4, Low-Emitting Materials: Composite Wood and Agrifiber Products refers to are particleboard, medium density fiberboard, plywood, wheatboard, strawboard, panel substrates, and door cores. The credit also includes laminating adhesives used to fabricate on-site and shop-applied composite wood and agrifiber assemblies. Excluded from this credit are non-base building elements such as fixtures, furniture, and equipment (FF&E).

To document this credit, the project team must provide a list of all composite woods and agrifiber products that have been installed in the interior of the building. The documentation must also confirm that each product contains no urea-formaldehyde.

30. EQ Credit 5, Indoor Chemical and Pollutant Source Control defines a dedicated exhaust system as an exhaust system (no return air) that creates the required negative pressurization to ensure that cross-contamination into adjacent occupied spaces will not occur.

31. The best approach to comply with EQ Credit 6.1, Controllability of Systems: Lighting is to categorize each space as an individual or shared multi-occupant space. The library will consist of many shared spaces such as conference rooms, classrooms, stacks, and reading rooms. In these spaces, the group must have access to adequate controls to provide functionality of the space to the desired activity. The credit's requirements do not specify a specific type or quantity of controls.

32. The spreadsheet should be completed as follows.

room	occupied floor area (ft²)	plan area of direct line of sight to perimeter visionglazing (ft²)	calculated area of direct line of sight to vision glazing (ft²)	horizontal view at 42" AFF (YES or NO)	compliant area (ft²)
private office 100	180	138	180	YES	180
private office 101	170	125	125	YES	125
private office 102	180	160	180	YES	180
copy room 103	135	120	135	YES	0
restrooms 104 and 105	410	0	0	NO	0
private office 106	180	132	132	NO	0
open office 107	2340	2270	2270	YES	2270
open office 108	1370	1260	1260	YES	1260
total (ft²)	4420				4015
percent of view areas	90.8%				

Private offices 100 and 102 were included at the full square footage of the office because more than 75% of the square footage in each office has a direct line of sight to the exterior. Private offices 101 and 106 were included at the actual square footage of direct line of sight to the exterior because less than 75% of the office has a direct line of sight. Copy room 103 and restrooms 104 and 105 were excluded from the compliant area calculation, as they are not regularly occupied spaces. The open offices 107 and 108 were included at the actual square footage of direct line of sight. Finally, because private office 106 does not have a horizontal view at 42 in, it was not compliant. After completing the chart, calculate the percent of view areas by dividing the total compliant area by the total occupied floor area and multiplying by 100%.

Innovation and Design Process

Note: The following Innovation and Design Process solutions are based on hypothetical project scenarios and were derived from researching past Innovation in Design Credit Interpretation Rulings. These suggested innovations have not been formally submitted to the USGBC for approval. Therefore, if pursuing any of the following innovations, it is recommended one research current Innovation in Design Credit Interpretation Rulings, or submit Credit Interpretation Requests to the USGBC.

33. ID Credit 1, Innovation in Design for Exemplary Performance, provides design teams the opportunity to be awarded points for exceptional performance above the requirements set by the LEED-NC Rating System. Exemplary performance ID credits are generally awarded for doubling the credit requirements and/or achieving the next incremental percentage threshold. Based on the project scenario, the following options provide two potential opportunities to achieve ID Credit 1.

Option 1—WE Credit 3, Water Use Reduction—Exemplary Performance: The project scenario specifies an interest in water conservation. An ID credit for exemplary performance for WE Credit 3 requires the project to exceed the base criteria (30% savings) for water use reduction by an increment of at least 10%, or 40% total. This credit is in addition to those earned for meeting WE Credits 3.1 and 3.2. Water reduction can be achieved by using low-flow sinks, waterless urinals, and dual-flush toilets. The project will need to calculate the interior water reduction and demonstrate a 40% savings.

Option 2—MR Credit 3, Materials Reuse—Exemplary Performance: The project scenario also indicates that the library will reuse the structural steel from a local bridge. An ID credit for exemplary performance for MR Credit 3, Materials Reuse requires the project to exceed the base criteria (10% of total material cost) for the minimum value of salvaged material by an increment of at least 5%, or 15% total.

34. ID Credit 1, Innovation in Design for Innovative Performance, provides design teams the opportunity to be awarded points for innovative performance outside of the requirements set by the LEED-NC Rating System. Innovative performance ID credits are generally awarded for comprehensive strategies that demonstrate significant and quantifiable environmental and/or health benefits. Based on the project scenario, the following options are two potential opportunities to achieve ID Credit 1.

Option 1—Indoor Environmental Quality relative to Toxins—Innovative Performance: The project scenario specifies that the city is committed to reducing toxins within the building. The design team will use alternatives to materials containing polyvinyl chloride (PVC) and polybrominated diphenyl ethers (PBDEs). The team can consider XHHN wiring and high-density polyethylene (HDPE) conduit, and limit other environmentally hazardous materials. For additional information, see the Washington State Toxics Coalition's website, www.watoxics.org, and the Healthy Building Network's website, www.healthybuilding.net.

Option 2—Indoor Environmental Quality relative to Acoustics—Innovative Performance: It is important that the acoustics in a public library are designed properly to ensure that an effective indoor environment is provided for the building occupants. The project team can submit a potential innovation strategy on meeting the American National Standards Institute's (ANSI's) acoustical standards to provide a healthy and comfortable space for building occupants. The project team will use acoustical paneling, soft surfaces, and additional insulation to ensure a high quality acoustical environment is achieved. For more information on ANSI standards, see www.ansi.org.